SECURITY AND CONTROL OF THE BUSINESS TRANSACTIONS (ASSET, STOCK/ INVENTORY & FINANCE)

...............GET RID OF THEM BEFORE THEY STOP YOU

ADETOPE ADENIJI

DEDICATION

The book is dedicated to the greatest security and control of the whole universe, and to the entire set of the individuals who believe in setting a paste to beef up the security and control in the organizations to have a sustainable and enviable organizations which however translates to the effect of the growth and development of the economy of the world.

TABLE OF CONTENTS

DEDICATION	2
TABLE OF CONTENTS	3
ACKNOWLEDGEMENT	4-6
INTRODUCTION	7-17
MEANING OF SECURITY	18-22
MEANING OF CONTROL	23-28
STABILITY	29-34
COMPETITIVENESS	35-43
ORGANIZATION	44-55
OVERVIEW OF THE ORGANIZATION	
HAZARDS AND THEIR CONSEQUENCES	56-147
THE PRODUCTS AND OUTCOME OF SECURITY AND CONTROL	148-184
AGENTS OF SECURITY AND CONTROL	185-209
TIPS ON THE MEASURES THAT ENCOURAGE SECURITY AND CONTROL	210-269
CONCLUSION	270-278
CONTACTS	279-280

ACKNOWLEDGMENT

My sincere appreciation goes to my family members, wife, child, relatives, friends and all the lovers of our books, services and musical initiative. To the schools I attended and the churches where the wisdom of God had been given. The box of my wisdom; The Very Rev'd and Mrs. J.A. Adeniji(rtd), Sir and Rev. Mrs A.B. Aladekomo, Baba and Mama Ayo Oni, The Very Rev'd(Prof) and Mrs Ayo Richards and hosts of the ministers in the sanctuary of God, all the teachers of all sorts of reasonable studies, men of humanitarian concern and other individuals of thought and values of the reasonable thought as catalyst to the growth and development of the world. I say thank you for the insight and your dearest support.

To my siblings, Bro Dapo, Segun, Wemimo, Oyinade and Florence, you are so precious to me. My friends that are uncountable in number in which thousands of the readers are part of, I quite appreciate you and your assistance. Mr Oyewo Joseph, who proof read the book, you are highly appreciated.

The church I attend at the moment, Wesley Chapel and every other Methodist

Churches, and all the churches in theworld, thank you all for the installation of the faith and godliness.

The schools I have attended, my teachers and colleague have impacted me exceedingly, lots of appreciation.

God bless you all.

INTRODUCTION

There was a particular point in time that selling of commodities and other consumables were sold on trust with the assurance that, if there is any defect, the producing company or manufacturer will make a replacement without much argument or stress. There was a time that, having oneself being involved in a mishap or accident that is insured automatically prompt the insurance company to react in accordance to their promise and agreement.

In Africa countries, there was a specific time period that the academics is being encouraged to the tune of having a guaranteed solid education for all the younger ones without the unnecessary stress of buying costly books and paying an exorbitant amount of money for school fees.

In the past years and time, many household do not border to close their door and windows just because they were assured of the prevailing security. While attempting to get across to your destination with the use of canoe, the first thing that rings in your heart must be safety. In a country or environment at which the security is porous, you may not find the individuals and the populace attempting to make purchase of goods and commodity. If there is no assurance of the security being in place, then what is the essence of the purchase of the varieties of the possession for safe keep?

It must as well be clearly stated that, investment is being attracted by the solid security and control. When there is an economic instability, political instability and uproar all about, the investor tend to have a rethought of investing in such an economy, most especially, the foreigners.

Knowing the state of the security of an environment at which a man lives or where an organization exist is quite very essential to reason above the purchase of immediate consumables and to think of the days ahead for the accusation of wealth, properties or investments.

Something must pre-empt another, such is the issue of the security to the furtherance and fortification of stability and continuous living. A perfect security leads to a peaceful coexistence, fortification and the strength ability to take decision that move both the individuals, organization and the world in holistic to the realm higher than just ordinary or imaginative.

Frankly speaking, security can be assessed in term of life, property, contract and agreement, job etc. But the factual and affirmative statement is that, in any commodity, contract, life and agreement that there is defect of secured environment or that its security is porous, there are thousands of dilemmas and disasters that emanate therein.

However, to quickly illustrate on the things that might be visible, the sets of point can be analyzed;

1. Extirpation and extermination- this is an act of putting an untimely death or stoppage to lives or organization, human or properties illicitly without no tagged punitive act or query to probe the act in question.

2. Wastage- this is an act of causing an end or termination to the existing resources, and yet expending on the

resources to have a control or gauge that can bring a normalcy.

3.   Pandemonium, disorderliness and discord- in a situation of insecurity and lack of control, people tend to react in an erratic mannerism and possess a distaste demeanor most especially among those who find it very complex to control themselves.

4.   Break of law and lawlessness- the already stated point look so interwoven, what this particular part is illustrating is the gap that exist between the normal and abnormal standard way of reasoning and reacting at the point of being defrauded or anticipating for a redress as

a result of been cheated. People move out of their right to intrude others of their franchise to live and to have their peaceful fulfillment of their intention and ambition.

5. De trust and disloyalty- this comes up often when a man discovers that he is operating at the state of insecurity. Here, there is no certainty and security on what he expects. This often translates to cheating or disloyalty in the sense that, the party trying to cheat another one knows that there cannot be any meaningful obstruction or interpretation or legal implication on his act. When people are not ascertained of their tomorrow or have believe in such an agreement they are found, they tend to

react in a way to cheat others believing that, if they are not too smart or swift, such other entity might defraud them.

6. Panic and uproar- apart from the sets of point mentioned, insecurity tend to bring unnecessary panic and intimidation to living, when one knows that any hazard or lost is naked or uncompensated. So also, at the point of agitating for your right or withdrawing the unlawful possession of what belong to you, it automatically generate uproar and waging war and physical combats.

7. Harassment and embarrassment- when there is insecurity, the rightful owner of a property can be harassed and

embarrass without the fear of law and the end result of what comes thereafter. There is always abrogation of power and the use of influence and status most especially among the elite and exposed.

8.   Robbery and stealing- a porous security tend to create a lope hole that breaks down the internal effectiveness of an organization and eventually leads to the absolute liquidation of investment and asset. At the face of insecurity, there is always issue of robbery and stealing which had made the growth and development in the context of the particular subject matter extremely complex to move further or for organizations attain their goal. This is often caused by the indolent assets or

human capital/individuals that are exposed to the sophisticated weapon to break in or by the lazy type that were only opportune to be employed or being made to handle the resource of an organization.

These and every other decadence are subject to the environment without the appropriate security and control, and this has made the subject matter very relevant to cushing the effect and proffer a substantial information that can impede the act in an organization, and fosters a better steps to the realm of expectation of all the organization and businesses of the world, most especially in a time like this that the technology is having a rapid growth, and that the juvenile delinquencies and atrocity are rampant.

However, to have a comprehensive elucidation and interpretation on the foresight and my plight consigning the subject matter and its affiliations, there is a very cogent need to define some words in both literal, lay meaning and the rightful consideration. Thank you.
Tope Adeniji.

CHAPTER ONE

MEANING OF SECURITY AND CONTROL

SECURITY-

Security is an act of going extra ordinary or beyond normal to have a precaution on an event that is at hand and that which one is yet to relate on. It is the creation of barrier on the pathway of the wastage or loop holes that can easily cause depletion or a halt on the path to record success. This is looking at the direction that ordinarily does not relate or reveal the immediate cause for it, but which is set to stop any deviation and challenges on the cause of having an injected unlawful contribution and destruction. Security is an action that thinks of the abnormality in the midst of normalcy to have a clue on how to curb the insecurity. It is an action that looks so disorganized but organized to challenge the fraudulent action and activities that are constituted by the illiterate but literate by position or qualification or privilege. It can be described as an avenue to curb the hazard on both present and the unforeseen circumstances. Another man can take it to be an attempt or preparation to take care of difficulties now and tomorrow or crushing the events of the difficulties that a human or organization can be exposed to. Another man can think of security as the measure of control and regulation that manages human behavioral pattern to discourage fraud and misappropriation of the resource and the material. It can as well be said to be the avenue of guaranteeing the end point of a binding agreement or lawful position of two or more parties. It can be termed as an act of checking the mistakes and errors on a particular assignment or attempts to evaluate its standard with the lawful precept and structure governing an individual, organization or institution in term of their contract, agreement and operations.

Looking into the fighting against the criminalities and lawlessness cannot be over emphasized as part of the security, since it is a means at which the violation of law and human right and order are redressed and protected. However, with the series of terminologies and definition that had been identified and deliberated on in relation to the subject matter, it is clearly not a controversial instance and issue not to have an elaborate information that can dwindle the prevailing insecurity in our environment, such that, a book on security and control of varieties of information and instances should be made and be promoted to have a check and balance that can lead to a thorough obstruction and end to the decadence of most of the organizational purse and investment creating a gap for the growth and development. Security should be an act of making a prevention and sometimes handling the defects on the stated guide line and misappropriation in the both the present and future context, whereas, control is the tool laid down to prevent the circumstances to spring up.

CHAPTER TWO

CONTROL

Most people consider control to be security in the whole essence, and they use the two words interchangeably, most especially by the set of individuals that find it very ambiguous to differentiate between the two words. Control is an avenue of checking or measure of looking into systematic operation that can lead to how hazards and depletion can be guided or eschewed in a given institution. These are the laid down procedures and actions that gates loop holes and the unlawful leakages in the resource in contrary to the potentials that moves into an action to carry out a full developmental intention and purpose. This is a stated opinion and guide lines and principles that adjust the limit of an individual in the organization, and stands a gauge on a certain standard or agreement to cause an action that can lead to the administration and management of the procedural intention and standard of the organization to be in place. Just said earlier, it might be ambiguous for someone to quickly administer the real meaning of the two words without a thorough understanding of their implication and application in the context of their appliances in the organization or institution. The main discrepancy can however be enlisted in the aspect of the tactical approach of the procedural stages to arrive at a stated pre tangential standard without default or compromise with the things that are not in compliance with the health of the organization, this simply means control, while the cause of an action to fight or attack the menace and hideous circumstance that might arise, in existence or that will come forth can be termed to be the act of security. The two words are always working together, used interchangeably and paripasu as some have concluded that, there is no differentiation in the words, but sincerely, when the words are critically studied, it will come to the notice that, there are quite difference in their meaning and terminology.

Security and control are however very relevant and compulsory in the day in day out of the activities of any organization and institution that look towards growth and development, and not that all alone, but that await the stability and competitiveness in the midst of the uncertainty and moving ahead of the other organizations on the same mission and objective. Without doubt, any organization that fails to have an adequate security and control leads itself to the path of liquidation and extermination at a very short time of its operations.

Conclusively, not all the management and proprietors are sometimes bold enough to handle the impact of the insecurity and control at their early stage, which however leads to a bigger issue in the subsequent years of their operations. It takes a man to be friendly, lenient and kind to have a meaningful outcome of his proposition and ideas while working with the employed hands, but there is need to have solid decision and stand operating unbent at the face of having a perfect security and control which will surely have the very best aftermath result and outcome that can lead the investment and organization to the stage of no limitation. A good security and control makes a good strength and fortification on the organization, individuals and contracts by making sure that the policy and condition in attributes to them are not violated or jeopardized.

Hence, the need not to handle the issues of security with levity in any manner; to affix the thorough minded and unblemished individuals to be in charge of the security and control of an organization. Any one in charge of security and control must be well tested, and must have a cleared record that cannot prevent him to expedite action that can lead to the adjustment of the abnormalities while his function is being discharged, and sincerely, a must for all the little lope holes to be patched and amended before they attain the stage of uncontrollable in their respective devastating effects.

CHAPTER THREE

STABILITY

There are millions of things that must be cross examined in an organization before it can be termed being stabled. The structure of the organization is never what count an organization being stable, neither is it how the service they provide looks like. A company may earn millions of dollars in a day, but yet termed as unstable because of its in-assurance to secure tomorrow or future. When all you possess or have are committed into the hands of the fraudsters, thieves or being proned to the insecurity, then, consider yourself having nothing if you cannot beef up the security and the control that can meet-up with the dilemma. A bad manager and officers can lead to a sudden emergence of severe waste and irreparable lost which can make an organization to lose her weight in term of resource capability and efficacy.

It is however concluded, that, the gap being created by either the internal factors or external factors is more very important to be cross checked at the point of checking for the stability or instability of an organization. An effective organization must be stabilized before it can be effective, competitive and efficient in line of its operational activities and purposes. Stability is the aspect of life of both human and organization that makes them to have all what it takes to move forward, not only that, but to ascend to the height of their expectation and destination. There is no way stability can be attained without having a simultaneous security that allows it to germinate.

A disabled pillar or set of pillars used in lifting and erecting a building bring an end to it unexpectedly and untimely, meaning that, when the pillars that are used to construct a structure are not strong enough, the expectation is to have a collapse, and this often leads to start afresh and again which however lead to more complication other than having a virgin land to be worked on.

To however have a befitting definition and ideology that can give a good terminology to the word stability, there is need to think in diverse manner to bring about the real picture in the mind and its application. Stability is the ability to withstand pressure or effect of the undue force that ordinarily should cause an impairment or total extermination.

Stability is an ability to regain control when a wrong step or decision had manipulated the already existing control to cause decontrol. It can be said to be the ability to receive and admit series of action and tension without being able to dissolve but to resolve. Stability is the strength ability to carry a heavy load with comfort and less stress with the absorber that balances it till they are consumed and overcome.

It is however very possible for an organization to be stable, and yet it is resting on the instability in term of the insecurity and lack of control, and the inability to make an edge way over the little issues which can cause jeopardy in whole lots of essence. The simple result of having stability on the instability is disability. It means that, the moment the platform or pavement a man or organization stands on falls off assumes the end point of the stability therein. Without a very accurate measure and tenacity to have a standard security and control in place, stability can be a bye gone or something that cannot be attained. However the needs for standard security and control to meet-up with the expected stability in the organization to grow and develop.

CHAPTER FOUR

COMPETITIVENESS

Competitiveness simply refers to a situation that arises as a result of evaluating what one has, how it can be used and probably challenges the already existing products and services. What makes organizations to be competitive can be traced to their uniqueness, simplicity, economic values, essentiality and significant contribution, durability, technological know-how, tactics and productivity in the midst of the other organization that are working together on the same terrain or platform. These sets of importance are critically examined before getting to a conclusive determination of the competitiveness of an organization.

It is possible for a certain thing to be in use for years or time immemorial without being able to compete in the global world, whereas, something very fresh and new innovation can be injected into the system with the highest degree of competitiveness. The competitiveness of the organization must never be valued without taking into the consideration of its status in the aspect of its global placement, positioning and evaluation. Just for an illustration, a telecommunication in a local area or in a country can be very competitive in its environment but yet having the incapacitation to withstand the other global evaluation yard-stick. This however leads to the deficiency in the outright competitiveness of such an organization in question.

Several are the football teams that exist in each country, and from time to time having themselves being involved in a competition or the other without the widely recognition and being able to compete with the other counterpart in the other countries. The whole lots of impression here is that, organization competitiveness must make it to be able to challenge and withstand every other organization of its nature in the other part of the world in holistic. It is very possible for you to be conqueror or flourish in your local area, and yet what you do is never enough to withstand the challenges of the others and being able to move over the initiation and the ideas within the country in which such an organization is found. The notion is that, though the organization is strong as termed, possibly because of the inability to have any other counterpart relating on the same issues or, because there is no other alternative to be used in replacement of what people can find around, such an organization can be so called vibrant without the proof and testing of its global evaluation which however depicts how competitive the organization is in its real sense. To determine the competitiveness of any organization, there is a need to verify its international position and make worldwide assessment. There is also a need to determine the area at which a man proposes or focus to relate on the competitiveness of an organization and the yard sticks that are in place to bring out the refined result. What I am saying is this, going back to the school days, there was always a dissimilar average percentages in use in a school to the other. Gazette for a pass mark in a school can be 30% whereas, that of the other school can be varied. Not to have a similar scenario, there is always a need to understand vividly the yard stick and the criteria to be exploited to justify the means and the end result. What I am saying is that, the grading operation that is obtainable in the global communities is quite very essential in deciding the level of the competitiveness of an organization, commodity and individual.

Competitiveness however means the ability to make use of the standard yard stick to measure the performances of the organization or to determine the phylum they fall into in term of assessment and result in their operations and the outcome of their service and production.

Competitiveness means the area and aspect of the testing of the strength ability and the effrontery of a system to check on its possibilities to withstand others in term of what can be produced, how well the world respond to their distribution and how good the condition can be to pass through the stages of difficulties and challenges. This is said to be a stage at which scope and value, sight cum ideology over speeds that of the others to query or challenge the optional desires and the taste of the world to gain or regain influence.

Competition emerges between organization of the homogenous commodities and services to serve as a determinant on the most viable and resourceful in the activities in which they are involved in.

The whole idea of the competitiveness and understanding the word or term is to understand and conclude on the very essentiality of the need to maintain an optimum value in term of competitiveness in other to be more proactive and upgraded in their mode of exploitation of their full potential to generate their services and product in a manner that command the global recognition and assessment.

To make a round up on the whole idea of information and elucidation of the competitiveness, without stability, there might not be the best testing ground for an organization to flourish or exhibit its full potential, which automatically have a full influence in the area of what emanate from such an organization, and turns out to be the basement for its competitiveness, so also, there cannot be stability without having an adequate optional value and a distinct proper standardized security and control to be the origin of the development and advancement of such a labeled organization, and hence, the issue of growth and development cannot be over emphasized when there is a standard security and control in any organization in question.

CHAPTER FIVE

ORGANIZATION

When one wants to look into the world of possibilities, there is need to have a good attempt to consider the word organization, and the word organize makes it up. Without a full interwoven of the varieties of the elements in life and working in synergy, there would have been a gap and a disjointed activities. To arrive at a perfect realm of the orderliness, there is always the essentiality of various components working together toward the same objective and purpose, and that makes a perfect system that can be in-formidable to penetrate into its optional values and pre tangential ambition. For an illustration, human system can be considered. One will clearly discover that all properties and elements are in charge to create a result and have an outcome. It might not be possible to close your eyes while you are looking at an object. The eyes are remained opened no matter what. While walking on the street, certain other important genuine ideas may run into your heart, and you may decide to stop on the initial ambition to attend to the new set of the conceived ideas, this simply means that your brain was not asleep while walking, and so on and so forth. These are what however bring about the completeness in the system of the action in the components that makes up human being. There must be relationship that is coherent and intact to function as one, and there is no other means to have it without having a sophisticated organization in place. The illustration is very essential, since you and I are enclosed within it. While I was working, I have seen someone being absinthial just because of having a nail issue. What I want to deduce here is that, whenever there is excommunication or fault in the body components, there is always distortion and dis-concordance which however affect the systematic functionality of the human nature.

Organization can however be termed as a system or coordination between the set of systems organized by the policy, vision and mission to work in the same alignment and direction to achieving a pre motive and a stated goal and objective to accomplish their economic expectation.

This is the arrangement of various units or departments that function as one to make an awareness and what they do noticeable to the world in order to most at times gain control, make impact, influence or gain their economic benefit.

Organization is an establishment formulated or organized for a specific function or purpose that is stated clearly what to accomplish with the stated mission, vision and duration of time period to make it materialized.

This can as well be termed to be an establishment accommodating diversified professional working together in line with the vision of the owner or the initiator of the idea to make abstract information a reality.

An organization must have all its component and structures functional and alive to live with. This means that, the inefficiency of the other element must have a defect and impairment in the functionality of the others, it means that when on is inactive or passive, the effect is adversely felt on the other structure working together with the defected one, and by so doing, it generates wide gap and vacuum if not well managed. This has however made it very imperative and crucial that all structures work together as one, and they are well performing to achieve a stated result and purpose.

These are the things that must be in operation before an organization can be made-up, they are the foundation and the bedrocks on which the organization is rested;

- Human capital- these are the set of the individuals that the organization make use to carry out their function and activities. There is never an organization that can be made to function in isolation or independently without the help of human being. Though, in some of the organization in the advanced world, there are many robots working, and they are more than the numbers of the staff of the organization sometimes, but there is no way there will not be human beings in charge.

- Resources- these are the set of the resources in use by the organization to create or to render their services and production of their goods and services, this can as well has to do with the initially mentioned human capital, commodities or services an organization operates on or with, e t c.,

- Capital- this is the life wire and the blood of an organization. They are the funds in use for the daily activities and preparation for the futuristic intention of an organization.

- Land- this is the natural gift and resource on which all activities are made. They are the areas encompass with the terrain of dry land, water and forest on which the operation of an organization is rested.

- Property, assets, office and meeting place- this is a place at which an agreement is concluded on as regards transaction and businesses, a physical structure might not be compulsorily involved, but a place at which people meet to finalize intricate views that can bring about the reality in their ambition.

- Coordination and control- this is an avenue to coordinate the entire activities in the organization, to direct, supervise and manage the set of functionalities that are prepared to make up a whole.

- Mission and motive- this is the compass and the directional pathway towards the placement and investment of all effort and contribution to have a conclusive result.

- Net-working- this is a means of having relationship and connection with the other organization, group of individuals and institution that might be willing to make use of the product and services being produced.

- Free entry and exit-to have a good and standard of operation, there must be free entry and exit by the member staffs and the external customers. This stipulates that, the organization is not a prison, and it is quite opened and fair in its dealing.

- Products and services- what this means is that, to have an organization, there is need to have a specific product and services being rendered, and this can be as a result of their motive and mission or rather organization focus.

- Management- these are the set of the group of individuals or proprietors that are charged with the whole responsibility of sphere heading the whole lots of the functionalities and activities in the context of the organization.

However, these are the set of the available structures on which organization are erected on, and to be candid, without having them in place, there might not be anything termed as organization.

An organization with a little of the security and control is exposed to a degenerating standards and prone to extermination. Therefore, the need for a comprehensive security that can make the system of the organization to work in a systematical and methodical manner; to bring about a concrete evidence of the proof of the intention of such owner or the proprietor of the establishment or organization.

Security and control are relevant to the increment in the value and standard of an organization since this generates stability and competitiveness that can affect the economic efficacy and benefit, while the organization tends towards its state and stage of reality.

CHAPTER SIX

OVERVIEW OF THE ORGANIZATIONAL HAZARDS AND THEIR CONSEQUENCIES

Sincerely, we have multiple of instances and issues that erupts in the various organization that needs a smart attention to be curbed and controlled. To some organizations, what is termed to be a serious problem is what they tap into to make a way ahead and to increase, so also, to another organization, what is made as advantage can be a reverse of what its effect is on another organization of the same purpose, but to be candid, any issue that is termed to be problems is problem in its area of identification.

It is also very important to know that, anything term as problem must be found an immediate and lasting solution to it not to collapse the structure of or the establishment on which they are apparent.

To however have an intense care and solution to the gaps and issues that rules the organization, or carter for a solution that can increase the wellbeing of the organization, it is very essential to understand the need to have a tidy up security and control to a large extent to avail the organization the true worth of its stability and competitiveness.

Hence, these are the syndromes that constitute gaps and instability which in one way or the other affect the growth and development of an organization when they are not attended to, or taken care of at the appropriate time.

- Lack of proper documentation, registration and receipt: the kind of activities that are managed in an organization is quite different from that of another organization. There is always the need to have the proper register that should be able to interpret the various natures of activities that are taken place in each organization to be able to have a remedy to the extermination and control over the hazard of insecurity and lack of control. To be able to have a complete provision of standard security and control in an organization, there is extreme need of checking through what the organization engages with, and to understand the different activities of all sorts that are being engaged with. This is the only genuine source to have a provision for the increase in the standard of security and control that anyone might think of. Some of the relevant registers and books that are very compulsory to the attainment of a tight security and control in an organization are; inventory/stock books, cash register, Creditors book, Debtors book, expense register, receipt, jotter for the sales personnel, movement register, warehouse movement register, attendance register, access register, e t c. These are the set of the register that create an avenue for the systematic provision for the guiding against the lope holes and all sorts of the decadence that are responsible for the degeneration and extinct of most of the organization in the world. When the due registers are in place, there will not be restriction on the need to move around and to delegate the work to the subordinates in order to be acquitted with the things in vogue and in operation. However, this then makes the issue of the security and control very relevant and compulsory in the global world while looking into their stability and competitiveness, and these are the topics to be deliberated on at the cause of our studies in the book.

- Organizational crisis: this is the issue of caucus formation or unlawful group that brings about an unnecessary uproar that can easily distract the attention of the management on given the best attention to the issues that can bring about the insecurity and lack of control. Also, when there is division in the organization, there will definitely be a division in the mode of operation and performances and working processing, which means that, there will be induction of delay and most at times destabilization and liquidation, so also, the security might not be guaranteed.

- Embezzlement- this is an act that has been in existence from the time immemorial in different organizations and the organization that are yet to be formed have all the tendency to be prone to such problem too. This is being intrude, injected and being carried out in the organizations by the unscrupulous minded staff or employer who believe not in what they can accomplish with their wealth of traits, sweat and have no believe in having a better future without being involve in the massacre, greediness and fraudulent act. It is an act of spending and using the money or properties of an organization in an unlawful manner either to gain or earn a personal economic benefit. It has to do with the sets of individuals that are working within the context of an organization. This simply means that it is an internal crisis which must be dealt with to seal off the loop hope that can cause degeneration.

- Fraud- this is an act that is quite synonymous to the issue discussed earlier. It is a way of utilizing the wealth and the resource of the organization for one's purpose without the approval or the authority of the organization in question. It is a process that dishonors the due process or approval to expressly seek for the permission of the authority or the management in charge before the materials and resources are used for such a person's reason. Sometimes, the money might not yet be spent, but mere going beyond one's limit and approval to either spend for a personal reason or even for the official reason pertaining to the organization might be counted as fraud. Making a replica of a signature to do a certain function if at all it is right and approved by the management, but due to a delay, the person in charge tend not to be available to append his or her signature, and because of this, another unapproved signatory appended his signature just for the sake of the activities to be undertaken, means fraud. Fraud can however be perpetrated by the internal or the external group or individuals that understand or get to know of the processing and procedures that lead to the stages of approval and cashing. When it is made up of a staff, it can be strictly referred to as an internal fraud, and when it is a fraud constituted by the external forces, it can be said to be an external fraud. Sometimes, fraud happens by both the two set of classes, that is, the internal and external, this means that this form of fraud has a backup of the release of the security information or act that makes the external party to pioneer and induce the fraudulent act. It is however pertinent to know that the 99% of the fraud are constituted by both the internal and external forces.

- 419- Though, this is often term as a slang, but in the real sense, it is more than a slang, and the meaning behind it is very necessary to be understood to have a separated meaning to the word 419. This is quite different from the word fraud, it is a pretense that looks to be true and real, and by so doing, a business is transacted on the false and fictitious information. This is when someone acts under pretense to act in order to obtain a financial obligation or collect money or other resources and thereafter disconnect. This can be identified as one of those things that are ruining and creating decadence in the world of the organization at large.

- Cyber café and electronics fraud and crime- this on the other hand is very differentiated from all forms of the fraud that had been mentioned so far, but very similar to the last one which is 419. In the situation of this, the person one is transacting with is not identified and seen or known, and yet, he is able to defraud the organization most at times. What this entails is the use of the web site of an organization to monitor the activities therein and to quickly find out the weaknesses of such organization to be able to make their way in. in the same vein, it is also materializes in a situation whereby, the codes or password of the organization is made exposed, and through this advantage, the codes are exploited to make a debit or purchase. These two acts have been very difficult to curb since the beginning of the technological improvement in the world. Funny enough, someone in another country that knows the codes and assess to your password can defraud you on the web site, and also, he may transact with you with the use of webcam, representing himself to be who is not till the fraud is perpetrated. This is yet another area to be extra ordinary careful on, when an organization is looking out for the maximization of all what it has to end up with the due growth and necessary advancement. This is however very rampant in the midst of the youth, that is juvenile delinquencies, most especially by the younger ones in the citadel of learning and unemployed.

- Extortion- not to forget the intention of this particular segment, I am only trying to list the aspects that needs maximum attention to close the gap of the insecurity and lack of control in an organization, and not only that, in the respective individual business finances. Extortion can be said to be a compelling act to collect money, commodity or properties and other valuable materials before something that ordinarily should be done can be done. Sincerely, it may come in any shape, this simply means that, the undue expectation of pleading before a work can be undertaken can be as well grouped under the tenet and parameter. Asking someone to get you a char set of pure water prior to arriving at the accomplishment of what ordinarily you are supposed to do can be attributed to extortion. Demanding for an amount of money to overlook possibly a crime or fault that should be reported or escalated can be termed to be extortion. Though, the effect is not directly immediate on the organization, but its hazard turns out to be very gigantic and uncontrollable eventually. What I am saying in whole essence is that, this kind of act should be dealt with accordingly in the organization because, by the time there is no room for such extortion any more or probably, the person that had been given the privileged is suddenly redeployed, there is every tendency of an act of criminality springing out in his character as result of the difficulties to manage himself with his income without such an avenue being created thereafter.

- Robbery- this is another very important hazard that organizations are prone to, and it is as a matter of fact requires a great concern to address the issue by making a solidified conclusion on what the measure of halting such a scenario can be before they are experimented or carried out. Robbery can be said to be an act of using a force or physical combat to obtain property, material, commodity or cash related.

Before one can categorize a case as robbery, there must be a form of intimidation with an object or sophisticated weapon to make a disagreed mind to concur and be willing to freely and voluntarily succumb to the treat and pressure by giving out his belonging. This act is very rampant in the world, and has being in existence from time immemorial. It is a means of chastising the real owner of the property to acquire it, and things that are used are cutlass, knife, sharp object, gun, physical fitness etc. due to these operations, many properties had been destroyed and wasted, billions of money had been robbed and taken away, and many more. It is however of great need to be prepared for the prevention of this kind of ugly circumstance than experiencing it before looking for the cure or prevention of its reoccurrence.

- Diversion of money or property- diversion of money or property can be for time being or for long time period. When one is cross examining the diversion for a short time period, a situation of making a public fund or the organizational fund to be fixed for a time period and to yield interest before they are used can be sighted as an illustration and an example of this kind. People tend to accrue wealth illicitly at the detriment of the other less privileged. In another language, when one considers long time conversion, one is looking at the misdemeanor of the staff or a delegate to make use of the resources or property by himself not for a while but for the futuristic purpose at the detriment of the organization or the other staff that are meant to be the beneficial to it. What I am saying is this, to have a good security and control in an organization, there is need to have an absolute eradication of this kind of uncalled for activities, this is because, these are the basis on which the insecurity and extinction, and liquidation of the organization are rested on.

- False accusation- here come another view that must be well managed to have a healthy organization. When there is no adequate security and control, many are the issue that rules around the four corner of the organization. When one says false accusation, it means an attitude that emanates as a result of getting properties or other uses with the pretense of actually acquiring them for the organization. In case, people purchase and acquire properties and commodity in their name on behalf of the organization, and thereafter make them to be theirs. Such a purchase or acquisition might be in connection with the prior knowledge of organization while the organization is having a pure interior motive and assumption that such an instance would not ordinarily possible to take place, or otherwise, it can come up as a result of blind purchase, which means that the organization did not know about the transaction at all before it comes to being. Well, what I am trying to buttress is that, in whatever way it comes, there must be a stoppage to a menace and the hideous circumstance of this nature that prevail in most of the organization which tend to reduce their capability and efficiency monetarily and financially to increase, and this can only be a thing of the past if only the security and control are in good order and fully in place.

- Job insecurity-in most of the employments, most especially in the developing countries, people have a conviction in exploiting others, other than giving them the right of the other to function in their capacity and earn what they have labored for. In many cases, staff of organization had been sub contracted to another organization that does not do any other thing than to cut out from the salaries and benefits of the others. Sincerely, if care is not taken, this alone can be a massive depression and dejection to the so called staff in such a circle which either make them to look at themselves as a second tier individuals in life or somebody that might not be able to apply accordingly into the system of the world in holistic without the job in which they have found themselves doing. What I am portraying is this, it is only a very few individuals that can manage this tense situation to become a real man, and at this face of this humiliation, the set of the staff enclosed in the bracket can be compelled or involved in an erratic demeanor and conduct just to overcome the situation at all cost, and for repositioning. It is quite essential to have a job security, when people cannot guarantee what the future can give to them, they behave in a disorderly manner, in term of being fraudulent and engaging in malpractices that endangers the advancement of the organization in totality. This and more other things are what the security and control should critically examine to have an enabling ground for the sustainable improvement in term of stability and competitiveness with the rest of the coexisting organizations.

- Credit and borrowing- this can be cross checked in two manners, that is, looking into the borrowing and credit by an organization for a specific purpose which is considered that it will generate back the money and the interest to pay back and to have a return that can be an added financial value to the organization.

Also, we have on the other hand, the company or organization that gives out credit and loan, just to assist the other organization to fulfilled their obligation and their capital projects, the intention of the organization is to give the credit facility out to be able to receive it back with the interest on it which turn out to be the company investment that takes care of the operations and other functions, and simultaneously to be the reinvestment. The impression here is that, when an organization either borrows or gives out credit facility without being able to repay or claim it back, they amounts to decadence and defect on the organization viability. As an organization willing to borrow or get a credit facility, there is need to understand the nature and the feasibility of the project it is investing on to be efficient to pay back. So also, when an organization is granting credit facility, there is need to understand the management of information provided and have a pre knowledge of futuristic event of the investment to determine if such money can be repaid back or not before making a decision or giving go ahead. The discussion so far still returns back to the issue of security and control management which entails the organization to consult either an economist or an accountant on business development plan, feasibility studies or better still to go for the profession courses and counsel that can easily take care of that in other to study the feasibility of the projects intensively prior to their time of commencement and operation. This aspect is as well very cogent and necessary while thinking of the necessity of security and control towards a stable and competitive organization in holistic.

- Care free attitude- many are the organizations that are ruined as a result of their care free attitude by their organizational staff and member. Too much of familiarity and relationship often lead to the care free attitude and being too loose not to know the limit or restriction of the customers in some aspects of consideration in line with transaction and operational activities that binds both the customer and the organization. We have encounter a situation whereby raw cash and instruments are left on the table while having a meeting with a customer, and perhaps, the staff has another thing to attend to, he left these things on the table, having the greatest assurance that the customer cannot perpetrate any fraudulent act just because he is well known by him or the organization. I want to say at this junction that, fraud cannot be carried out without having the whole information and gist that leads to it. In another consideration, take for an example of a control that is violated just because of the intimacy which had led to a severe lost. The vault key should be managed by two individuals for the control sake, but instead, because of the intimacy and friendship, an officer felt comfortable to release his key to the second officer, and in each a time this happens, the one that goes in all alone removes out of the higher denomination that are loaded in the vault. This was continuous and constant till the auditors came around for the scrutiny and check-up which however revealed the gap in control and security which ordinarily should have prevented such scenario. What this analysis is trying to say is that, transaction and function should be well guided under the stated security and control that is made up by the organization to have a guide and adequate prevention that can tighten up the gaps that might arise as a result of a porous insecurity and lack of control through a care free attitude.

- Carelessness in the use of password or revealing password and pin codes- the use of passwords and coded number for the use of ATM cards and other transactions are very essential as this can be a measure to wage war against the indiscipline and financial crimes in the organization. This serves as control measure to the entrance, collection and approval on the electronic uses and means of identification and possessing the authority and accessibility to operate on a transaction or movement in the office area. However, some set of individuals often give out their passwords and codes to the other people just because of the trust and the level of familiarity which however generate issues eventually. So pathetic and very sadden that, most of the so called reliable individuals are the cause of the calamities and the fraud the organization witness often at times. There is extreme need to have a fore knowledge of what password and pin codes mean before they are initiated or given out to the member staff or any other individual that should be responsible for its use. Ordinary password to the door must be well kept to prevent the unapproved individuals to gain access to the entrance of the restricted area of the organization. What this means is that, password should be handled as one's life and death, this is as a reason that, whenever there is any fraud emanating or coming forth on the password or the pin code, no one cares or want to know who made use of the password, what happened or who was responsible or how it came into being than to pass all fault to you as the authentic owner, and at the same time, to be liable for the consequences. An intensive finding may allow the fraudster to be arrested or questioned, but that has nothing to do with the due punishment as regards the error that has been made. It is however very essential for the security and control to be very intact to oversee the issues that might be in connection to the lope holes attributable to the carelessness of the pin codes and passwords.

- Exposure of documents-it is not a news or new thing anymore that most of the staff handle the customer's transaction and documents with levity without minding who has an access to it. Documents are meant to possess their confidentiality and secrecy from the external bodies and the internal individual that are not approved to have access to them. Things like customer's mandate, signature, address, phone numbers, email address and all sorts must not be made to be exposed unnecessarily. Sincerely without the clues on the customer's package, there might never be a fraud on it. What this implies is that, there must be someone, somewhere that must have given out a reliable information before the evil of defrauding an organization or customer could come up, or possibly, the customer also had erroneously careless about his information. It is however very essential to understand that document are to be well kept and covered when having an affair with the third party. This will however obey the rule of the confidentiality and secrecy of the information that the customers are entitled to, to receive from the organization, and when fraud is prevented either on the customer's account or in the organization, the clients and the prospective client finds it more confident to relate and to do business with such an organization.

- Know your customer (KYC)- just as said, know your customer or KYC is something that most of the organization handle with carefree attitude, and this had landed many of the existing organization into an enormous problems and issues. When one says know your customer or KYC, this does not mean that, it is the only the external customer that should be well known, but the internal customers must as well be well known too. I have had an organization who does not know the residence of their staff, the question remains that, in case of any issue, how can the staff be traced out? There is need to know a bit of all the individuals working in the organization, if possible to have connection with their family, by so doing, this will surely reduce the risk of fraud and if there is any, it will not be difficult to get such an individual that had engaged in such a mediocrity act. Just same way it is very important to know your internal customers, it is as well very important to know your external customer. When someone is well known by you, it will be very difficult for such an individual to cause you any harm. This is because he knows that you have all his details, and not only that, but that you know him in and out very well, and the set of the individuals around him, therefore, it might very slim to see such an individual or corporate body to think of fraudulent act. This must be part of the security and control that should be in place to have a drastic reduction and if possible, a total eradication of the risks and danger that are uncalled for.

- Mismanagement and waste- mismanagement and wastages is one of the vital significant issue in virtually all the organization that have contributed immensely in a negative way to the wellbeing and the promotion and increment of the standard of the organization. In this consideration, there is nothing like fraud or theft, but it is merely gross indiscipline on how to make use of the available resources and materials possibly because of the excessiveness or surplus availability. One of the most degenerating factors that stand as the destroyer of the organization remains the mismanagement and wastages, and they tend to bring organization to a sudden halt and liquidation. These can come in diversified ways, such as waste on electricity, use of paper, use of water, diesel and petrol, being not economical and other ways. It is indeed however very crucial for all to know the essence of management and preservation of the organizational resources and material towards a sustainable condition for the organization to gain its full potential of stability and competitiveness which however reveal the standard of the security and control that is made available in the context of such organization.

- Limit- this words simply means that, there must be a specific function and the range on which each of the staff can relate on. There must be a kind of control that stipulates what each an individuals can do or the decision they can take in each a condition of activities that emanates. To further explain the whole idea, it means that, if one is a cashier, there must be a specific amount he must not exceed to pay without the notification of another higher officer. This officer as well must have his own restriction also, and other officers irrespective of their position till a certain amount that the management can decide on. Limit in the capacity of the staff is very necessary in the sense that, they serve as a means to control the issues and hazards that are meant to erupt ordinarily. It prevents people from being too exposed to the risk and the hazards of the job, and as well serves as security and control to patch the lope hole in the finance and cash related activities in an organization. This however simply reflects the crucial need for the notion of limit to be in place for the organization improvement and increment.

- Availability of bags, purses and personal belongings in the work environment- sincerely, one needs no one to reiterate the disallowing of personal belongings in the transaction areas. Apart from the disfiguring of the work place, there can be mix up in the placement of the products, material and resources in a wrong place. Take for example, set of chain belonging to an organization can be placed in the personal bag unknowingly, and if care is not taken, if such a product is already in use at such an individual's home, the mistake might be slim to be rectified. In other way round, the personal belonging are the main source of the tool that most of the fraudsters make use of to do their havoc and unruly contaminating activities. If you came in with a bag in the money environment, and everybody saw you with the bag while coming in, then, at the exit point, if 10,000.USD has been stolen and kept in the bag, no one might challenge you or have the envisage that such an exhibit is kept therein in the bag most especially where people live with optimum trust.

However, this can lead to colossal irreparable loss most especially when the person in question disappears as at that moment. Therefore, personal belonging are to be restricted and prevented to manage the huge risk that can be generated when the security and control are exempted.

- Partitioning and demarcation- having an office that is not well partitioned or demarcated might lead to a factor that can increase the hazard in the organization. It is very expedient to partition or demarcate an office to improve on the security and control of such an organization. Though, some organization believes in the transparent inter relationship and business nature, this can be made to work out by the use of glass to partition the office, which means that, though, the set of the individuals working together are very transparent in their dealing due to the transparent demarcating glass being used, but the door can still be looked or covered to prevent all the documents around the corner of each of the offices confidential and saved. An office must be well partitioned and demarcated to have a guide and sincere control that can make a reduction in the level of the problems that can surface in the organization.

- Figures and words- to mention the various issues that arise in the aspect of the security and control might be very tedious in the sense that, as one is being considered another one emanates. I am only of the opinion here that, most of the staff and the agents of the organizations do fail often to be careful about the amount in figure and words which however generates an unnecessary issues that ordinarily should be eschewed. The similarity and the discrepancy in the amount in words and figure are very spectacular issue of concern when it comes to finance and its concerns as any variance can easily lead to a very expensive error that might be toughed to the corrected. Better to however even try to be center minded on the amount in words other than the figure. This is because of the weight of the amount in words compare with the figure in the consideration of the financial transaction. What this means is that, if the actual amount of consideration is 500 dollars and the amount in word says five hundred dollars, but the figure reveals 1000 dollars, and the amount that the customer parted with at the point of collection is 1000 dollars, then the simple outcome of the event is shortage of 500 dollars which must be rectified by having a replacement or running after the customer for the adjustment and rectification. It is however very important to pay attention to details at the point of having issues to do with the finance as this has contributed immensely to the gaps being created from the time immemorial, and many other organizations will still continue to be involved in such a circumstance due to the lack of the adherence to the laid down principles and values that are meant to be followed to prevent it. The amounts in words are always weighted higher than that of figure at the face of law. However, this saga can be control when attention is given to the adequate perusal and scrutiny of the figures and words before the transaction and before the transaction begins.

- Date and time- this are another very important and very cogent aspect that must be given a thorough consideration to. What this means is that, there must be coherence in the particular time and date that the transaction of a particular customer is carried out to be able to do the tracing and follow up when there is a gap. Some organization use time stamping machine which is already made up of the time and date on the crone of the machine which stamps the document with the inserted removable plate or rubber with the date and time respectively. However, in the case of the organization that are yet to be matured to the level of having a machine to do that, it will be advisable for them to cultivate the habit of writing the date and time on the documents, this is the only thing that can allow the systematic trace of the transaction should in case there is an issue to be corrected or there is need to have a reference subject to the transaction. This however interpret that, there is a very serious need to have both the time and date inscribed on any document that is taken or treated. This also attribute to the issue of security and control in the life span and existence of the organization and in their convenient manner to resolve issues in whatever way they might come or arise.

- Identification and signature- the whole essence of this particular point is the avenue to know who is who and to have a trace to the root of issues. To consider the first word identification first, this can be categorized into two ways, that is, cross examining the issues of the identification and checking the particulars and the addresses of the customers. Making sure that all the documents and every other things that relates to the information that connects with the names, occupation, identity cards and every other relative things must be well confirmed for a proper identification and KYC purpose. Another aspect of the identification that is very vital to mention is, the identification of the staff and others in relation to the organization, each an individuals must be well registered and must be well identified with each name and not only that, there must be name tag or identification card that must make each an individual well known separately and reveal their names. Each a man must be well identified and known to be represented at the point of honor or punishment. So also, the issue of signature, there must be a particular signature for each an individuals in the organization, and if peradventure there are some signatures that are very closely similar, there must be need to have a change on them so as not to have any signature that looks so alike for the sake of a distinctive separation and attribution of a signature to another individual. Signature and identification are however very essential and important to be well managed and properly handled to have the deepest of the information that can lead to the very beginning of the customer's genesis and foundation, staff different distinctive separation and different signatures that can easily analyze and identify each of the staff that have appended them.

- Customer's instruction- the customer's instruction is quite very relevant in dealing with them and handling their transactions. Each of the customers have what their requirement from each an organization is, and this is just their expectation to retain and have them with the organization. Customer instruction at the point of having them into the organization formally or receiving them with any form of recognition and dealing with them can serve as a control and security measure in the sense that, it comes to an inquisitive issue to examine when there is variance in the demand of them customers. Customer instruction is very pertinent and of high value when it has to do with the nature of the services that one should provide for them and how to go about making it a worthwhile since the human desire and wants are insatiable and can never be similar. In all the mission and vision statement of all the organization, one will see that the intention of the organization to maximize their potential and value is centered on the customer's services and satisfaction, and that is the most reason why their interest must be the priority and major concern to have a fulfilling and perfect mission and vision accomplished. In the light of this, the desire and interest of the customers should be very relevant in the area of performance and attention of the organization to have the best of the standard that exist between the organization and the customers they have. So, as I said initially also, this also serves as a means of having a due security and control on the issues of the demand and request of the customer in a protected and secured manner to attain the ultimate desire of the organizational purpose.

- Cash, document and commodity in transit- these are the set of operation that are yet to be completed or gotten to the last resting place. It is an exercise that entails the movement of resources, documents, materials, commodity, services or cash either in a physical operation or abstract. Often at times, most of the organizations are involved in the series of the operations that leads to this from their respective places to the consumers arm's length or convenient places. This is to make the consumption and uses of the product and services very closed to the customers for their uses and distribution. There is however the need to consider having a tight security and control to be able to guide and protect the valuables from the interception of the fraudsters, arm robber and hoodlum whose interest to strike through the gaps is their focus to access the resources that are not well protected and secured most at times. What I am saying is that, the issue of the adequate security and control to make the documents, products and service to be well kept is very important to ascertain the continuity and the consistency in the service provision and the going concern of an organization. It is however very necessary to give a due attention to the issue of the cash, document and commodity in transit to have the expected dream of the organization being fulfilled and attained. Any resource that is exposed to the hand of the fraudster, arm robbers and hoodlum might be a waste or negation that might not be regained.

- Use of safe and strong room- Frankly speaking, there are many things that are nonchalantly considered very relevant in the organization that have their respective functionality that cannot be well over emphasized or with. Such is safe and strong room, most especially for the organization that handles customer's documents, valuable and physical cash. Some of the organizations do not have a sacred and specified place at which their valuable are kept which often make them to be prone to the hazards that comes thereafter as a result of this. Safe and strong room are described as a place where valuables can be temporarily kept or put before the onward movement to the right place of safe keep or financial institution. It is very mandatory for all organizations that deal with the document of the customers, most especially the documents that need to be well secured, and their valuable to have a safe and strong room for their security and control. No one is contesting or contending on the issue of robbery cases that had led to the opening of the strong room and the safe, but the issue is, it is not all the operation of the attacks on the organization with safe or strong room that is at all times successful. Many are the cases of the armed robbers attack that had led to their arrest and capturing them just because of the time delay at the point of opening the safe and strong room, and when such operation arises in the mid night, where there is no one to inform them of the control on the way in, it becomes more cumbersome and time wasting, which had made some of the robber to run against their luck. The suggestion is that, it is mandatory for a safe to be made available in a work environment and organization not only to prevent the arm robbers, but to keep some salient information and valuable material away from the member staff that are not approved or given the right of the authority to have an access to such an information or precious commodities that were kept.

- Bank confirmation and notification- it is always very necessary as a matter of fact to make an instruction with the bank to confirm instruments and transaction before they are been given. There must be a tight relationship with the bank or your banker on money related issue or releasing of the commodities in charge of them, and it must be very constant and regular to avoid fraud and a parallel transaction to occur on the organizational transaction. Whenever there is any information not confirmed, and it moved into your record, there is need to query the approval of the transaction, sincerely, the organization can request for the refund and replacement which might not be needed if the transaction is genuine. But there must be severe warning so as to prevent such in the nearest future to have a standard security and control in place for the prevention of the opening for the bad ones to strike or have interference. The confirmation can be in place in a schedule to reveal the total transactions that are coming forth in a week so as to have the pre information and knowledge of what the expectation of the organization A,B,C to Z looks like, and at the same time, to have their request and confirmation well files or recorded in their respective files. This can be information via the internet, intranet, phone conversation, sms, physical document etc. The idea of the confirmation and notification has however contributed immensely to the security and control that exist in the organization.

- Call over and proof- calling over and reconciliation are both similar term that have a closely representation. Calling over is an act of looking through the work that has been done on a daily basis after the working hour. This is done by printing out of the journal entries or the transaction captured to verify them with the physical instrument in term of the figure that was posted, amount in word and figure, date, signatures and every other thing that has to do with the customer's mandate and instruction. At the point of doing this, the incorrectness on the tickets and instruments are generated and extracted to be rectified immediately with the approval of the authorized approved individual in charge or to meet with the initiator if essential, phone call can be made to make an appointment with him either immediately, following day or as concluded. On the other hand, reconciliation comes often in a month or monthly basis. This is an act of making sure that the total summation of the postings into the general ledgers and other account were actually well posted. In case of disorderliness or incorrectness, the correction is pointed out and rectified accordingly. These are just the measure to look into the entire activities that have taken place in an organization by each a member that was represented on posting or recording with their identification and proof, to ascertain that all the posting and registration during the month are accurate, and were posted into the right account as specified to have a balanced account.

- Reconciliation- reconciliation is another aspect of security and control that is very vital to have a good accounting principle and good security and control to be in place. The issue of calling over and proof have to do with the internal processing and confirmation of the entries that were posted into the account of the organization, whereas, the issue of bank reconciliation has to do with the relationship of the organization with that of its banker. This is an avenue to check through the activities in the account of the bank in relation with the organization and the actual transaction that the organization carried out, being expected to reflect on the account. These include the un-cleared transactions and cash in transit. The whole essence of this is to be sure that there is no wrong posting, that transaction the bank's account reveal is appropriate and without no error, the charges are in line with the concession approved, there is no double entry of the same transaction, and to ascertain that the account of the organization is balanced compared with that of the bank record. This is very relevant to cross examine that there is no strange transaction that move in during the cause of the posting and acting on the activities of the organization, and if there is any, such must be reversed and corrected. This is another means of security and control that is worthwhile to be in place for a good organizational growth and development.

- Numbering of transaction- the number of the transactions that takes place in an organization is very relevant to ascertain how many transactions are dealt with in a day. There must be identification number for each a transaction to make it traceable when there is an issue emanating on them. This can easily depict the numbers of transaction in the system compares with the available ticket which however comes first with the exposure of the instance of the issues in organization. When the numbers of the ticket is more than the imputation, it ordinarily means that, some of the tickets have not been posted or probably, there are some of the postings that did not reflect in the system through the system failure or aborted transaction. When the figure of the ticket is lower compares to the system's figure, what this means is that, there are some fictitious information and posting which were carried out without ticket or there must be transaction which was double posted.

In the whole essence, the idea of numbering has helped times without number to excavate and escalate issue that has to do with the security and control, and times without number, such issues were found having a solution to them.

- Asset counting, labeling and registration- asset management is quite crucial in an organization to have the full detail of the numbers of the asset that are available in a specific organization at a point in time. It is an avenue to give the full detail of the total unit of the asset that an organization possesses, and to categories them into various classes as designed by the organization. There is extreme need to know the number of assets, to be able to relate on the ones that are good or bad; to know when to acquire more or dispose the old ones. Also, asset counting and registration makes the labeling of the assets and identifying them either by marking them or pasting signs on them well registered on the asset management register. As soon as there is any misplacement or theft, the actual asset that is involved is quickly well identified and traced out. Since, enormous fund is spent on the assets of the organization; there is always the huge essentiality to know the position of the assets because of the value placed on them. However, asset counting, labeling and registration is one of the aspects of the organization that most of the organization have not been looking into, which however constitute to the regression and fund wastage in such organization. The assets are meant to be appropriately managed till their values are fully expended, and they are turned to obsolete.

- Inventory/ stock counting and management- just in the same manner that the assets are counted, there is importance to have the commodities and stock well analyzed and to be well managed before any business that is involved in the market of anything commodity can survive it. A business operating in the service rendition does not need stock or inventory management in such a manner at which someone selling commodities such as shoes, clothes, electronics, wines e t c. are in need of it. Though, there is no organization that will not be in need of this service or management in the sense that, there must be set of the commodities that are kept for the future use of any stated organization at a point in time, in a place referred to as either store or safe. Inventory analyzes and stock analyzes make the position of the total commodities and prices in the store to be known without much stress. When there is a document or table that reflects the position of the business, there is always a reduction in the theft or unapproved removal of the commodities in question. Some people believe in the amount of money they give to them rather than being to detail on what constituted the money. In such a scenario, the sales personnel might be selling and earning above what they return back to you without being able to confirm it, and this amount to loss eventually. Inventory or stock management is quite very pertinent than the issue of money related matters, without these commodities, there might not be any cash returned at the cause of transaction, just as there might not be returns without services in a servicing organization. So, there is need to venture into the management of inventory or stock to make the due profit and to overcome the issue of fraud and theft that might have been a deterrent to the increment and upgrade of the organizations. If any organization desires to move ahead or to grow and develop, there is need to pave attention to both asset and inventory management. When there is a good chart indicating this, there can thereafter be an avenue for growth and development of an organization. Most of the infant industries complain of poor growth and development, there might not be any without the proprietors being able to free themselves, to know things that are current and in vogue, so also, to carry out their marketing strategies either in light or elaborate way.

- Use of ultraviolent light and mercury- the use of the ultraviolent light or mercury light are very essential to combat the issue of the fake instrument or cash of all kinds. Any organization that has as its function to accept any kind of instrument or physical cash must make the availability of the ultraviolent light and mercury light to be in place. This is for the confirmation of the genuineness of such instrument or cash at the point of accepting them and treating them accordingly. A clone cheque or fake note that is taken by any officer is a negation to the purse of the organization, though, such officer must be liable to face the consequences of such admittance and acceptance, which means, that by the time the fraudster or the perpetrator of such an act is away, the person that received the transaction and acted on it must be punished, penalized or repay accordingly. Scanning can only be done by the person that understands the basic features and characteristics of various instruments and cash, aside these, the scanning might not be well performed under the mercury light. Unlike some of the testing machines, immediately the instrument or the cash is inserted into the machine, the machine automatically accept or reject it. The problems associated with most of these machine is however that, when a note or instrument is mutilated, the machine often rejects which however leads to manual testing and this entails the proper familiarity and being inclined with the characteristics on the instrument and cash. A cash and instrument that are well scrutinized and perused will never form a shortage or have any defect on the appropriate transaction or contribute any havoc of any kind that can lead to fraud or regression.

- Update and adequate documentation- a good documentation is always very advisable when there is need to have any dealing with any organization and individual. This is because when comprehensive information of an organization and individuals are taken, it leads to the ability to be able to make a finding before transactions are stated, and if by any reason, there is an error, it will be very easy to have a remedy giving to such. There is no way that one will talk on the proper documentation that he will not mention the issue of the identification that was mentioned beforehand. The set of things that can make a comprehensive documentation are always obtainable in the bank. These are among others, the certificate of incorporation, form 02 and 07, identity cards, utility bill, bank statement, and more others. These set of the documents are very relevant to make a new organization or individual that is attempting to admit a new customer irrespective of their size and what they relates on. Having the needful in place will however serve as a security and control measure that can reveal the very beginning of the transactions and transactions in case of any issue to be resolved, most especially when you are dealing with the activities that has to do with exorbitant amount

·

- Dual copies of transactional document- in many of the banks, the standard is having a posting copy (bank copy), the customer's copy and control copy. This is to have a full control and evidence to proof the transactions. It means that, for each a transaction, the organization has a copy of each document, one is for their reference purpose and the last one is for control purpose, which means that, it is reserved for the auditors and other financial individual that are assigned to peruse the account of an organization. I am only looking at having at least dual copy. Hence, a copy goes to the organization while the second one goes to the customer. If the processor fails either knowingly or through human error not to post or treat the transaction, the customer's copy is with him to make a claim or to show that the amount is paid, while the issue will be resolved during the audit. Any copy that is duely stamped and appended a signature is authentic to make an amendment in case of any error. Security and control however are very relevant to reduce the risk of the unscrupulous hand and officer in an organization.

- Report of shortages and overages- mostly, the staff of the organization find it difficult to report their discrepancies in term of shortages and overages. It is however part of the ethic of a disciplined mind and a thorough representation to reveal such. Most people think that, with the fact that they have shortage in the time past, they are the owner of the overages that comes out of their transaction duties. It is very inexpedient and unpopular to have difference in the book of account or any form of transaction without the report on it. Candid, it is never ethical and can be referred to as stealing in its interpretation. The finance department must be fully educated on the ethics and the value of transparency when comes to the finance of an organization. The drilling, awareness, and seminar might be actualized but the aspect of security and control must be thoroughly examined to have a closed lope holes. It is never a crime to have difference in the finance, but it must not be rampant. Also, when it occurs, it must be reported, else, it becomes a punitive act. This is one of the important aspects which must be well perused to have growth and development, mostly, at the lower level of the operations in the infant businesses.

- Personal observation- all what I have mentioned is centered on the ability to have a strict focus on the result of each testing. Being observant creates an ability to carefully make decision that does with what one is doing and being able to understand and notice things that happens around him. Without serious observation and attention, all effort on security and control might be aborted. Personal observation and due attention might not be well over-emphasized in the issue of security and control. There is a saying that, prevention is better than cure, prevention of an event is quite more important than having a solution to it. For an example, a fake note was taken in as a genuine note, however, after the customer had gone and the officer was about to close his financial book, he discovered the fake note. The point here is that, the deed had been done, and such a scenario might not be apportioned to a specific individual or customer since it was unnoticed at the right time. If such a note has been noticed and returned immediately, that would have saved the wastage or shortage. What I am saying is that, personal observation is quite relevant to the issue of security and control, and must be dealt with reasonably. Anyone who is either directly or indirectly connected with the cash or cash related must be mentally, emotionally, and physically set to prevent its hazards other than having solution to them after the deeds have been done.

- Numbering of instruments- it is most often discovered that the instrument in use as receipt and the posted document are not numbered. When there is no security or control on the document used for either the external or internal purpose, there is often a lope hole created for fraud. Take for instance, on a cheque book, a leaflet is tore in between the booklet. The owner of the cheque can easily identify the theft at the point of looking through the booklet, and when instance of confirmation from the bank is required, he might be able to stop the fraudulent perpetration. Also, when a bank post with the sequence number of the cheque, the system automatically alert the processor at the point at which the leaflet is jumped through the transaction history. It is however very expedient to have a control and security in term of numbering on the instrument for both the payment, receiving and posting purposes. However, having distinctive information or labeling gives the alert to have a direct connection, trace and sometimes to have a stoppage on kinds of fraudulent acts which might be aiming at conquering the existence of an organization.

- Draft/cash and transfer acceptance-I am only trying to look at the instances of insecurity towards the acceptance of cheques. Many organizations have liquidated just because they received the dud cheques from their unscrupulous customers. Draft, cash and transfer are the best measure to relate on whatever form of transaction as far as the developing countries are involved. This is because most of the developing nation do not count any meaning are such to the criminality act of issuance of dud cheques. Not until there was a promulgation of a law in respect of the term and condition for the punishment on the dud cheque in Nigeria, the criminal act was rampant. Organizations are however strictly advised to attune to the collection of draft, cash or ask their prospective and incumbent customers to strictly adherent to such a transaction of same kind. When a draft is issued, it means that the account of the bank that processed the draft is already debited for the amount overleaf, which means that, the instrument possesses the same value as physical cash. Such instrument can never be returned from the clearing house without having the equivalent amount in your interest. Though, the receipt of the bulk amount must also be prohibited. Any amount above a reasonable amount should be referred to be paid into the bank for security reason. Any paid amount should be confirmed by your account officer or any other officer in charge before the release of the products or services. If at all, the customer paid in fake notes, and the bank accepted them, that should not be your own problems than to have value. Making use of electronic transfer is also the modern way of payment, and it must be adopted in the transaction of an organization. If at all, you have no account in the customer's bank, he can always make use of NEFT transfer with a very little amount to make such a transfer to the bank of his choice. When you have an account in the same bank with the customer, it makes it easier in the sense that, a cheque can be paid into the account, not only that, there is a transfer form to be used for such a circumstance. Since virtually many attempt of having other payment like promissory notes, cheques, credit e t c has failed, then, there must be thorough check up and carefulness for the desperation to sell or doing customer service at the detriment of liquidation of an organization.

- Cashless transaction and economy- this is the kind of economy that operates outside of physical cash. Most of the developing countries are just imbibing this, but the pathetic aspect of it is that, most of their policies are contrary to the principle of cashless economy. The entire value of the net worth of an organization is loaded on the card. Transfer is however made through this card to the tune of the owner's interest. Passwords and code are generated for the owner of such a card at the point of carrying out any services of his interest. The hazard of it however that, if the keyword or password is exposed to an unapproved person or fraudster, the entire money might be wiped off without any form of approval. Though, this is the recent and modern style and very convenient, but it has a colossal disadvantage when there is a lope hole or when error erupt, which might lead to total lost. Very advisable to all to get attuned to the operation of card use because a time will come that there will not be physical cash transactions in the whole world, and to be very careful on how the pin codes are used or if possible to change them often. However, electronic cards are made for thousands of purposes, but the aspect of security and control can not be over emphasized, and the security and control on the card are as well very expedient to guide against financial havoc.

- Use of biometric doors- biometric doors are made not with the usual key, but one must place his fingers, identity card or punch in a code on a specific portion of the door, and the door recognizes the impulse of the fingers, card or figure to open the door. Without having an access or being configured, you can never be allowed to move-in, else, someone approved must assist you to open such doors. The doors are made for the restriction of crowd to the confidential arena or cashing area. The good part of it is that, there is registration for all the movement of all sorts of individuals which makes it quite easier to trace issues. Use of the biometric doors and gadget in the organization can not be undervalued or worthless to have a good security and control. Organizations are however admonished to grow in line with the technological improvement to work in the same alignment to the improvement in the global world to have a standard security and control that can lead to stability and competiveness.

- Periodical check-up- there is need for periodical check-up on any obligation that is designated or apportioned to any individual discretion other than the owner of the business. This gives the report and result on each position of the cash related issues, and it must be carried out when the people in charge are not noticed. By so doing, many irregularities are discovered and detected by the system control. Issues like borrowing from the organization fund before pay day, unapproved credit, facility to the customers, illegal transaction on currencies, shortages and overages e t c can be up-rooted. A good organization must however make room for such a habit to examine her staff and the operation efficacy. Very possible that the cash in the vault is tampered with, but without the confirmation of the entries and books, it might never be revealed.

This manifests the hidden secret of an operation staff most especially when he is caught unaware.

- Periodical staff transfer/movement- no one is an island of knowledge. There must be periodical transfer of staff on a desk to another in the organization to change their habitual relationship or ways of reasoning and hidden things. When a hand or staff is changed, issues are escalated because someone that is coming into the office will not want his or name to be tarnished. A cleared table must be aimed at to start afresh, however, transfer of staff have brought about issues and make the long lasting havoc to be exposed. Therefore, the issue of transfer must never be toyed with to have total in-depth information of various desks.

- Armed security for cash in transit- cash in transit is the cash that are on the progress of movement from a place to another. It means that they are already out from a place, but yet to land at their destination. Lack of security is however associated with the instances of armed robbery attack that had claimed thousands of lives and valuables. There is always the need to have a full provision for the armed security forces to move at all times with the cash in transit to be able to avoid the interception of the gun men or invaders most especially when it has to do with a normal routine activities irrespective of the worth of the enclosed money.

- Stand by armed security in the organization- in case of any organization that is involved in collecting of huge amount of inflow or revenue, there is need to have a provision for the armed security that can scare away the interest of the robber in such an organization. They must be at a hidden place where they can not be numbered or exposed to where their form of ammunition can be valued. When there is information of the presence of the security men in an organization, there will be limitation in the attention of the robbers to the organization. Many organizations would have been robbed, but due to the presence of the security men, they have spared. When a mad man sees gun, he recognizes it, not to talk of the mentally aligned human. Armed security is relevant most especially where huge amount of intake is received for the purpose of bit of security where a worthwhile amount is received.

- Cleanliness and tidiness- there must be conducive arena for the cash and cash related transactions. Many records of cash shortages and overages, loss of document e t c have been attributed to the uncleanliness and untidiness of the environment at which transaction is taken place. I have witnessed an un-posted document being extracted from the waste basket as a result of being packed with the dirty papers, I have seen bag or envelop being mistakenly thrown off as dirt, e t c. the point is that , when the arena is cleaned, the risk get drastically reduced. This however increases the security and control in its little avenue.

- Use of camera and visual gadget- to a very great extent, the use of camera and visual gadget have assisted on the issue of security and control. This is a means at which the entire environment is placed under surveillance by the use of camera that is connected with a screen on which the total activities can be viewed. The use of this means has however contributed immensely to the security and control in the organization, in the sense that, most of the atrocities are noticed prior to their time of execution. And sometimes, when they are carried out, camera avails the security intelligence the due information to make a trace on the incident or occurrence.

The little points aforementioned are however the things that is extremely required to pay attention to in any organization that looks towards a better tomorrow and greatness. If all the stated information can be clearly dealt with wisely, there will surely be a better improvement, growth and development that are competitive in the organization that pays a full attention to them and handle them with the utmost concern and seriousness. These are however some of the salient point that are very crucial in nature when considers the stability and competitiveness of the organization in the world at large.

CHAPTER SEVEN

THE PRODUCTS AND OUTCOME OF SECURITY AND CONTROL

Candid, having a tight security and control are very necessary for the increase in any organization one may consider to attain the apex level of the order, and to be represented in the midst of the other viable organizations. Any organization that toys with the issues of security and control is tending towards its sudden liquidation. It is the life wire of the organization that must be handled with all strength, might and full courage to attain. Security and control connotes positive shift of an organization and guarantees consistencies and the assurance of the continuity in the operation of an organizational operation.

It is then very necessary to have an organization that has its functionalities working for her but not against her focus or purpose. When there is difference in the expectation of an organization and its end result, then, it means something is not appropriate and must be adjusted to have forwardness.

What I am looking at in this segment is the benefit and advantages in connection with the security and control. I have enumerated few of these, and they are thus follows;

- Peace and harmony- what does peace and harmony means? This is a perfect coexistence in the midst of the staff members or the workers in the organization. It is a state of calmness and tranquility in an organization as a result of what happens therein. Peace and tranquility are measurable, and can be evaluated in the sense that, when it prevails, its evidence must be vividly seen, and when not, it must be also noticed. One of the measures of peace and harmony is therefore security and control, and it must be dealt with diligently to translate to peaceful and harmonious environment. To therefore have a stable and competitive environment, there must be a sophisticated security and control that is alive to the tune of provision of what it takes to have calmness in the organization.

- Assurance of tomorrow- when there is security and control in place, there is every tendency of having an assurance of tomorrow. This can be viewed at the angle of good thorough accounting practices which makes the security on the finance very comprehensive and thorough for expansion and enlargement of such an organization. When an organization is dependable enough to checkmate all her lope holes and all forms of financial decadence, then, the probability of continuous existence and her ability to take care of her staff members are ascertained. By so doing, more strength will be given to the work to do, and not only that, but there will be sense of belongingness to assignment in place which directly or indirectly affect the nature of the products and services, and not that all alone, but the development and increment in the organization as whole.

- Growth and development- growth and development are the increase and germination in the part of the organization or the entire whole of the organization. When there is a positive change in a part of an organization, it is termed to be growth, but when there is an entire change in the organization, it is termed as development. While looking at the general overview of growth and development in an organization, the issue of security and control are very crucial, to be tested and critically examined. Just as discussed, tranquility and stability are very essential to the expected degree of growth and development. No single individual or group of individuals or organization can move ahead in the midst of pandemonium and confusion. Therefore, one can simply make improvement, security and control are however the invisible and visible source of growth and development.

- Economic stability- economic stability can simply be regarded as the stage at which an element, individuals, organization or other entities attain the ability to withstand the pressure of disability on their pathway to their destination or making their interior motive to work accordingly to have a symbolic effect on the economy of their residence. Without the stability and balancing, there might not be improvement and upgrade in an organization or any other kind of industries. To however understand what economic stability means, one must be able to identify what stability connotes, and not only that, but what economic means. Economic stability can then be said to be the stage at which an economy of a state or nation gains full control over the deficiencies that can be an obstacle to her growth and development. In term of fluctuation, inflation, deflation, employment, regression, e t c. which could constitute the highest degree of the epidemic impact on the economic. This is an avenue to create and recreate a sustainable and worthwhile future that can hold the destiny of both the incumbent generation and the generation unborn. This is when the whole lots of the activities in the economy can work coherently to make a distinctive effect that can leads to advancement in all classified values of the expectancy of the humanity. This is a situation at which a little effort generates huge returns and whereby any form of injection into the economy commands feedback and returns. The issue of economic stability is indirectly or directly affected by the security and control in the fragments of the organizations in a specific economic boundary and country. Since the productive, servicing and creativity activities of each an organization form the basis for the economic substantiality and stability, then, the issue of security and control must not be handled with levity in the organizations to have its immediate impact on the economic stability of the economy of direct its discussion.

- Organization stability- one might most likely understand the point better when it is studied before the just concluded sub topic, economic stability. Organization stability can be regarded as the ability to wax stronger and improve in the midst of the prevailing destructive agents and circumstances. To have a stable organization, there is need for a thorough security and control that can withstand the rigor of destabilization. When there is stability in the organization, there is a fertile land to erect structures of various kind of projects, and to do exploit that can work in concordance with the pre-tangential motive of the organization, but this might never be accomplished without the security and control.

- Expansion and extension in the investment- security and control contribute to the increase and expansion in the investment of an organization in whole. When there is increase, growth or development, the revenue and intake of an organization expands. If the revenue of an organization is enlarged, this automatically leads to the increase in the net profit, which thereafter allows the owner of the company to re-invest part of the profit back, which thereafter envelop to increment in the investment. Also, in case of a company that issues shares to the public, when there is expansion or the populace can sees that the organization is well doing, they tend to be comfortable to risk their money on investing on such organizations. Investment can be termed as an act of putting or committing certain money into a specific project or purpose for the interest of having a due return or percentage on the money, while the value of the actual money kept is un-changed. The point is that, no investment can grow or expand without the due consideration of the factors that encourages it, and such factor that must be well considered is security and control. This is however to say that, growth and development in the organization have a long impartation in the investment of an organization.

- Increase in the work force- we have agreed that, development and growth are only in connection with the security and control, therefore, any organization that expands or develops in structure is as a result of the security and control. One quickly recognizes advancement in an organization at its physical evaluation and assessment. When people discover that an organization is fast moving and the staff are growing and well paid, this tend to attract many more employees to feel like being part of the success and to move in the same trend with such development. This then attracts many applications for the few jobs which allow the management to have diversified choices of selecting the very best hand in the midst of the numerous individuals, man power and human capital that have applied. Organization does not work, and might not be able to create a name for herself, but the good hands deliver the great work that makes a great organization. The best hands that are selected will automatically leads to the blast and the general outstanding performance of the organization to attain greatness. Security and control can however lead to this when they are in good position in an organization.

- A good projection and view- when there is good security and control, there is always a good projection and views coming out in an organizational schemes and managerial decision. What this means is that, when an organization is in good order or healthy, it will have strength enough to have the best use of her managers to get the best vision, view and projection. Any organization without vision and good projection ends up at a state of getting not to her destination. Security and control make up a distinctive provision and special reaction to the formulation of policies which can thereafter lead to the competitiveness of such an organization that can come forth with something substantial out of nothing.

- Orderliness- one of the best product that security and control can bring about is orderliness in the organization. There will be at all times respect for rules and order and the other provisions that are guiding the life of the managers or the employees when there is solid security and control. Orderliness in the organization means respect for the provision of laws and policies which when they are violated are punishable. Orderliness is quite substantial to have forwardness in an organization, and to have a perfect outcome in the organization preempted issues. There must be cadre in the abrogation of power, giving of order and authority. This sequence must then not be violated at the point of dishing out the due control. Without a due control, each man may decide to function in their capacity, which means that, no one is responsible for another. The point is this, to have orderliness, the chain of control from the managing director or the management to the last ranked personnel must be separated and work in synergy to accomplish the same purpose. When the control is intact and interwoven, there will always be avenue to have a competitiveness and stabilized organization.

- Mannerism- both orderliness and mannerism are closely related in the sense that, they are both in relation to the pattern of acting or relating with the official activities of the organization. While the orderliness relate with the adherence to the professional standard of discharging responsibility, mannerism has to do with the manner of behavior or disposition. When there is tangible security and control in the organization, it often leads to a better manner amidst of the employees and the way they carry out their functions which automatically have impact in the efficiency and expansion of such organization.

- Freedom of expression- this is an act of being able to have freedom expression or to have a closely related heart to heart discussion on the issues that can bring about enlargement and add value to the organization. The employees are often very free to express themselves when things are in good order and the security and control is ascertained. Freedom of expression is quite very important to receive a feedback from the set of individuals that works with an organization. Without this, organization might not be able to understand what the employee's expectation and grievances look like, also, the organization might not be able to check the impact of the policies and information passed across to her staff. Free flow of expression allows both the organization and the employees to understand themselves hitherto, to have a coexistence that can make a reasonable outcome. The term freedom is the avenue to make or pass across or show forth the feeling by an individual in the organization which might have no binding effect on the management or organization. It is however noted that in the organization where security and control are lacking, there might not be room for such an instance of freedom of expression which may make an increase in the gap of the relationship and interconnectivity of the organization and the staff members.

- Equity- equity means given attention or consideration without being bias in judgmental verdict or response. It has to do with justice and fair attitude in relating with the people. It is an act being separated from partiality. When there is equity in an organization, it means that the organization can see beyond the ordinary relationship or transaction to relate with both the external and the internal customers. There must never be consideration that gives preference or difference to an organization or the other, individuals or the others, e t c,. This means that, the way a company A is attended to must also be the same manner of being attended to the company B to Z. The technique or approach must be first come and first to be attended to, not having a special personal interest that may violate the term equity. Also, in the context of the organizational matters, there must be free hearing in any issue erupt. The policies must be well treated and administered to affect the clients of the organization equally. At the point of giving bonuses, allowances e t c. the interest of all must be taken into full consideration instead of having a restriction. It however means that, the issue of security and control must be well managed and attended to prior to having an equality and healthy relationship standard that can make an organization to effectively attend to all issue of their clients equally.

- Use of initiative and creativity: When one looks at the word creative and initiative, the simple analysis means, the act of using one's innate composition and ability to make decision, to act in a certain manner, to bring about a unique invention or discretionary decision. This has to do with the internal genius of efficiency of man to instill into the world what has not been in existence or develop what has being in existence, but to have a new shape that counts it to be updated. Sincerely, each a man contain in him the efficient capability to react in a particular situation when he or she is enveloped in a situation to use their discretion. When a man is not given such a permission to use what he has, what he has can not be tested, not only that, it cannot be experienced. There is a saying that, the best of the opportunities or changes lie in the ones that are yet to be recognized and tap into. This simply means that, the technology and discovery of tomorrow will without doubt be more sophisticated than that of yesterday and today. Without given the due attention to the people on how they should or can use their inbuilt natural talents, their real personality might not be discovered and one might not be able to evaluate the prevailing policies, to be upgraded to match up with the immediate need of the people. It is however noted and crucial to have a standard security and control because without the security of job, and knowing that the management will not condemn and prosecute a new vision, the mind that can think of improvement or giving a due attention to advancement might not be willing to do so, so also, when there is no control, there will definitely be a limit to the level of performance of the staff, which means that, they will be regulated before their intention are put into their active practices, this may lead to fruitless contribution and inactive decision in the entire organization as it may be.

- Improvement in the standard of living: Candid speaking, not until a man have a stable employment or engaged in an economic activity that can set him free financially, emotionally, and physically, he might not have an improvement most especially in his standard of his living. Improvement in the standard of living can simply be said to be a stage at which a household gets to the level of its maturity, to blend up, to manage the defect of the economy and live a standard life, though not surplus, but to be able to live comfortably in the midst of instability and irregularities. This is a situation at which household can fetch for their daily needs and desires e.g being able to feed themselves whenever they are hungry not necessarily 3 square meals, ability to pay for the service charge, that is , NEPA, water rates etc. accommodation, rent, owing a house or shelter, ability to move around, not necessarily to have a car, but to have the provision that gives the privileges etc. In the presence and the paste of security and control, it is very important not to do away with the increase in the improvement in the standard of living of the certain number of the representative of the household involved in the specific organization under the due consideration, and sincerely, the issue of adequate security might not be undermined.

- Organizational standard relationship: a standard relationship within the organization can never be at the face of uproar, chaos and discord. This means that, for organization to attain her peak of operation and full exploitation of resources and what it has, there is need to have a cordiality and tranquility prevailing in her arena of operations.

There must be a relationship which can work together from the bottom to the head to fulfill the provisional information of the organization. This increases the productivity level and gives the sense of belongingness. When there is flop or issues that can be resolved by someone else, they get it done without checking or looking for the others who is responsible just for the forwardness and growth and development of such an organization. Things tend to work in synergy to have a good end result. A good relationship and rapport make an organization to be very rapid in its response to improvement and growth. It allows the systematic operation of the organization and an orderly coordination of such industry. A perfect relationship leads to a free flow of communication and operation which will definitely be apparent in the life of such organization. The issue of free communication from top to down and down to top just discussed in the cordiality in the relationship of the individuals and members of the organization is apparent; a free communication from the higher hierarchy to the lower point and vice visa cannot be far-fetched in the sense that, the relationship is tight and cordial. We have recorded thousands of cases at which the security guards and cleaner in an organization had served as an agent to the prevention of life and property of their organization. In the face of standard security and control, that allows the staff to have the due sense of belongingness and being applauded and celebrated on the little contribution and impart to the organization, they simply considered themselves to be in the system at which they operate, and hence, it gives them the pride to have a contribution even at their lay angle of development which can be refined and made to be a standardized tool of moving the organization forward at the long run. It is however noted that, security and control are quite very essential to be in place to have an arena that necessitate the free communication in an organization.

- Transparency: This is an act of making decision to the organization and purpose being known, not to the entire staff, but through the grape-vine sometimes, for the member of the staff of the organization to be in the light of what the intention of the management looks like. The management can only be transparent in their ideology and decision when they know that, things are in good shape, that is, they have reliable and trust worthy individuals. Sincerely, there is no need of going through the face of having management meeting in the mid-night or in another secured place when all the staff is reliable. And this can only be traced and evaluated based on the past experiences of the organization. What I am saying is that, the staff is meant to be well taken care of in term of their salary, bonuses and other benefits and job security. These are the set of values or elements that thereafter gives back to the organization in return and in term of their level of efficiency, going extra mile to deliver, loyalty, trust, pro-activeness and so forth. It is however noted that, transparency also have a lion contribution to the well-being of an organization, which means that, when there is security and control, there will definitely be room for transparency and advancement.

- Motivation and Inspiration: When there is perfection and absolute positive staff in the life of an organization, it simply means that the set of the individuals are attuned to the peak of given the very best of themselves to the positive shift in completeness of their purpose. Motivation and inspiration are both seen and unseen factors that gives the right sense of having an urge for better performance other than what had been recorded in each a state or stage of functionality. The staff can be motivated and inspired by the conducts that were stated before-hand in the subtopic ahead. It can surface out in the working conditions, salary, wages, bonuses, allowance, annual leave, travelling bonus, upgrading and promotion, measure of performance and prize giving, management relationship etc. These can serve as an avenue to encourage the staff, which thereafter leads to the stage of doing more and competition among the staff members. Also, management as a result of the maximum security will tend to produce more of the product and services since they are sure of the security and provisions for them. When the security and control are well in place, this gives the owner of an organization the courage to make more activities that can be beneficial to the organization to happen, and at the same time, the aftermath result cannot be far fetch on the staff of the company. When the management is motivated or inspired, the member of the staff of the organization are also impressed and taken care in term of money, conditions and other policies of the organization. It is however necessary to know that, an organization without a good measure of security and control might find it depressive to have motivation and inspiration in existence in the context of its operations, which directly or indirectly affected the organization revenue and finance.

- Trust and Reliance: Whenever the security and control of an organization is in place, in good order, there is always trust and reliance. This means that, the degree of relying on the others and believing that, though they are not there, their interest must definitely be protected as a result of the security and control in the organization is visible, guaranteeing of personality: Most at time, our working environment remains the place that most of our time is spent and consumed. Therefore, whenever there is need to have a confirmation of character, demeanor and other attributes and dispositional values, the organization and individuals prefer such to be done through the organization one had worked or he is working. When the security and control of an organization is well and alive that no fraud or diversion of resources had occurred, it will be very easy for the organization to give a very good and supportive recommendation of human's character of their staff when they are still with the organization or after they might have left.

- Exposure of the strange and hideous acts among the member of staff: In case of any occurrence of strange and hideous acts at the lower level or at the stage below the management level, if the communication within is free and the relationship is cordial, such a disrepute intention or act that might bring about disability or liquidation to the organization must have been mention unofficially to the organization management staff members. This however is possible only when the interests of the employees are well taken care, and their cares and concern are paramount in the system in which they operate. There is a need for a standard attention of the management on the well fare of all the staffs to enhance the type of security and control befitting the organization. When the staff are well managed, they tend to be involved better in the aspect of the security and control at the level that the management might not be able to see, which means that, the staff become their law abiding agents in charge without the involvement or little involvement of the management.

- Focus in the organization: When one says focus, it means an atmosphere that does not have a discord or distraction that can make people not to have a due concentration on the motive of their priority which is services, to attain a common goal of the organization in term of customer service and productivity to meet the standard product and services yard-stick that can lead to competitiveness and stability of such organizations. When an organization is having a focused group, they tend to go extra mile to make the perceived impossibility happening. There must be an environment that is out rightly focused to make an impartation that can lead the organization to the very stage of their expectation. A focused environment brings about a genuine worth of human efficiency into practice and experimentation. A focused organization can achieve at a faster rate than unfocused organization in all areas of evaluation as a result of the cordiality and relationship that brings about unity in existence and application of their pre-motives and insight. An organization that is not focused will definitely be looking for the fortress and strength ability to move forward and relate at the realm of its full exploitation and productions. There cannot however be an organization that is focused without the present of a thorough security and control. This however stipulates the need to be thorough in an organization to have an extra ordinary performance and to have paste ahead of the other competitors or the other organization in the same bracket of operations.

CHAPTER EIGHT

AGENTS OF SECURITY AND CONTROL

I have been discussing on the term security and control in the book, but yet to give a clue and preview of the agents of security and control. It will be an unforgiving crime to go ahead without having a brief pause to give a meaning to the subtopic at hand. Agent of the security and control are the set of individuals, or other entities that makes the security and control to manifest or undertake. What I am saying is that, the security and control can never in existence without the contribution and effort of some entities and human contributory factors.

This leads to the issue of who are the initiators of security and control, who implements it, who evaluates its value on the organization, the motive behind it, on what is it meant to be actualized? These are the series of questions that must be handled with a very great concern to understand that, the responsibilities are leverage not on the ghost or invisible entities of the organizations but by the people who are the decision making bodies of the organization.

These are the set of individual that are involved in the provision and implementation of security and controls;

1. Employee: These are the sets of the people one works with or work with you. The very last individual in an organization, which can be the messenger is not excluded in the term and quoted employees since, he receives his payment in the organization. Anybody that has his name written on the pay roll of an organization is a qualified employee of an organization irrespective of their status. Sincerely, without the set of individual that are made use for the activities and functions of the organization, there might not be a vast contribution or impact in the progression, in the sense that, the owner might not be able to solely accomplish the

task up to 1% value. These are the machinery and human capacity being used to deliver the expectation of the organization in form of services and production. These individuals are quite very essential in the aspect of security and control at their respective level of operations. Security and control tend to be applied at the various section and level of the organization, and these can be handled at the very level at which each of the employees operates. When the security and control is failing at the lower level, the organization has already failed, this means that, if at all the employee of an organization comes together to be one in a difficult tense situation, the problem and issues that the organization is looking at resolving might be accomplished. To then have a dependable employees, it is a must to learn on how the welfare of the employee is made the chief priority of such an organization in question. It is however not possible to have a security and control of the best standard without the contribution of the employee or having the due employees of an organization into full discussion.

2.   Management/Employer: These are the ruling body of the organization. It has in its bracket, the managing Directors, Treasurer, secretary and every other individual that are decision making groups. The management set the policy of the company, they came up with the strategy of achieving it, they employ the staff, they create series of unit and department for the actualization of the functions, set the standard for security

and control of an organization and thousands of every other thing that affect the organization in a positive manner. Any blame or lope-hole within the organization falls on this set of individuals, and that is the reasons for their uprightness and disciplined personality that must be able to act in accordance to the structure of the lay down policy and rules and regulation governing the organization. There is no way one will then relates on security and control without the availability of the set of individuals that are made to make decision and implementing it. How thorough the management of an organization is, contributes immensely to how the wellbeing of an organization looks like. When the head is defected, the other part of the body will definitely suffer it. There must be a good leadership that can withstand the defense of the creativity of their idea, and to make it standard under all forms of favourable and unfavourable circumstances. The agent of security and control in an organization can not be well termed or defined without the due consideration of the management of such an organization.

3.   Customers: Without customers the organization stands to gain nothing. Customers are the king and the main motive of the institution or any organization. These are the set of individuals that are responsible for the activities and function in an organization. Sincerely, if the organization has only one or two customers, there might not be the need for the owners to employ staff to

accomplish the task ahead, and sincerely, the tendency of having such an organization in consistency for a long time period is not ascertained if the commitments of such customers are not adequate. Customers are the very beginning of all functions in the organization. This means that, if at all you have a good service to render and products to sell, and you have no customers, it amount to nothing or vanity, but the presence of the people who came around you to cherish and to patronize you for the service you have to render and the products to be sold respectively brings about activities that emanates to selling and buying, and reproducing more of the services and product to the very taste of state that can meet with the style and choice at hand or in vogue. The very genesis of all transactions however depend on the customers coming in before you can be engaged in distribution, production, movement, loading, buying raw material, having employees e.t.c. The set of activities that emanate between the organization and their customers however bring about the exposure to the document and finance of an organization in which the unscrupulous and fraudulent minded penetrate most of the time the fraud occurs. Customers, being so pivot in the organization making, should be made of great importance to the organization, and to understand that all organizations are in the business for the sake of the customers. If this is now the source of the organizational strength and competency that it is very crucial, well noticed and genuinely considered while having a construction of the organization foresight, then, there must as well be an adequate security and control measures that can be applied to manage their presence in any form of organization accordingly. We have experienced the customers defrauding the organization, owing an organization without payment, revealing secret on the tactics of the organization system and control, misleading for their personal gain, e.t.c. All these buttress to the issue of security and control that the management must be set to have an everlasting solution to for the consistency of such an organization, guiding against the lope-holes that tend to drop the capability and the efficiency of the organizations or to exterminate the vision of the corporate and individual forecast.

4. The shareholders: The shareholders are the owner of the company in the quota of their shares and the percentage to their interest or investment in the organization. These are the set of individuals that stood to share the burden and the ownership of the organization as a result of the declaration of the ownership of the company during a very huge and giant project or when the organization conceived to upgrade or enlarge her financial potency, and they issue out shares of certain unit to be picked up for the value of the financial investment as shareholding. The contribution of the shareholder is his right of order to being part of the owner of the organization. Also, the shareholder can

transfer his obligation and shares to another person if the share is transferable. By the virtue of buying shares without being part of the organization from the inception qualifies one to be one of the appropriate owners of such an organization. The directors are however being selected out of the shareholders, and this is strictly based on the percentage of their contribution or shares. The directors work on the interest of the other shareholders of the company in a completeness of its legality and the provision of law and legal document as stated by the owners of the organization. They have the right to remove the management member when they discover that they are not performing or inactive. They decide on the matter that can improve the effectiveness of the business in which their interest is invested, and also look into the activities of the organization therein. There are different types of shareholders, and they are only liable to the nature of the share they possess. Since the interest of the subtopic is to study the agent of security and control, our discussion will be minimal on this topic, shareholding, but I will like to clearly state that, since they are enclosed within the management of their investment and liability, it is a must to thoroughly identify their contribution and importance in line with the security and control of an organization.

5. Nature of the policy within the organization: The nature of the policy in existence within the organization has a

greater role to give and to contribute in line with the security and control of an organization. Any organization that needs the best result, not only in the aspect of the security and control, must have a solidified policy in use. This is a policy that controls the affairs within the context of the organization in term of the regulation of the activities within and the behavioural pattern of such an organization with the world in holistic. The type of policy in existence has a magnitude of value on what an organization looks like. This serves as the element that propels the action and reasoning of the organization member towards the direction predesigned in their formulated policy. Any policy that is not standard enough ushers the abnormality of the organization to be clearly expressed in form of their existing values and relationship with the other organization and individuals it has to do with. However, to think of the security and control, it is very vital to look through the phase of the policy of the organization to understand clearly of the lope holes and the nature of the system in the organization that can promote and sustain the security in its general connotation. When one thinks of the policy in the organization and institution, the aspect of the gauge and control in line with how money are to be spent, the approved signatory and authority to any instrument, the limit of amount of money to be approved by any of the signatory, when should a company considers selling shares or going to the public, method of stock control, what binds the staff with the organization, directory on how the nomination of the authorized signatories should be selected, stock taking and every other important things in the aspects of not only security and control must be well understood and analyzed. This however makes the policy of the organization an instrument to the growth and development when the security and control of an organization is searched into.

Hence, the policy of an organization is referred to as one of the major elements that connote a good measure of sound security and control that can easily lead to stability and competiveness among the other global organization in the world.

6. Implementation of policy: When one reason on the policy without its implementation, it looks like dreaming without fulfillment. In the time past, there are numerous of versatile ideal, and sincerely, these could have caused a tremendous change in the nature of the world in holistic. The inability to however implement these policies or put them into action has however made no impact or relevance on the intention. It is a good thing to have a solid and sophisticated policy made in an organization, but it is something else to make use of the policies judiciously. Irrespective of what the nature of the policy looks like, implementation of the policy matters. Without the due implementation of the

policy, one might not know how good or bad it is. There are thousands of thought and anticipation that are very splendid and awesome when one views them at the reasoning realm but they are distaste to the nature of the world, things around and intention at the point of application. What a man can perceive but not demonstrated are always very good when it runs through if I had known I would have done it! The action not undertaken can not be as valued as the one you had taken. An action must follow a view to be able to evaluate what it worth. In relation to the subject matter, a policy must be implemented before it can be felt. A policy made without being implemented cannot have any meaningful impact on the status of the organization. The essence of the policy is to create activities and to showcase the guide on how the set of the activities can be regulated and directed. Having a policy of a standard nature is important, whereas, having no implementation of the policy is like not knowing about it or having such a good idea. However, it is a must to know and understand the need to have an accurate implementation of the policy of the organization, to affect the views and proposition of such an organization in line with their intention. To however have a working policy and effective policy, there is need to have its implementation on the course of the organizational series of endeavors in which the security and control cannot be underestimated or understated.

7. Government Concern, Regulation and policy: This are the sets of the involvement of the government to ameliorate and ease up the condition around the organization activities in which both the property, material and cash control and security cannot be over emphasized. Under this condition, the government looks at how the security and control of her economy can be attained to have a system that can lead the institution and organization within its context to the stage of growth and development. Some of the areas at which the government had reacted to the issue of security and control lie within,

1. Control on the issuance of dud cheques: this made it very cumbersome

for any client or customer to issue a cheque without having fund in his account. In a scenario at which this is noticed, it attracts a severe punishment and penalty.

2.   Cashless Society: This is the decision of the government to eradicate the use of physical cash within the system. This saves the rigour of moving large amount of cash from a place to another or having such amount in the company or an economy.

3.   Policing and Security Guard: This is an avenue at which the government produce the agent that stands against the insecurity and fraud. This set of

individuals interfered into any criminal and fraudulent activities. Within this context, we have police officers, we have judiciary and the laws enacted for the break of the law and regulation. This has its contribution to the control and security when the offender or someone that thinks of such an act knows that there will definitely be aftermath result or consequences on any contrary or inappropriate act undertaken.

4. Punitive act on crime and frauds: In the analysis above, the aspect of judiciary was mentioned. There is always a standard punishment for the offenders and violator of rules and regulation in connection with fraud, theft, 419 and

every other punishable acts or misdemeanor.

5. Cash Limit: This is not only applicable to the bank or the financial institution. it is an aberration and violation of rules of law and the policy governing the organization to have huge amount of money or receiving such from their clients or customer without its onward transfer to the bank as soon as it clocks a certain specific amount, and at the same time, to make provision for the armed security officer within the area or compound of such an organization or communicate with its banker to come for the conveyance of such fund to their bankers.

6. Technology and Invention: This can simply be regarded as one of the salient agent to the control and security in an organization and the global world. Technology and innovation have brought us to the state at which without moving an each, one can see what is going on in another country. Right away from your closest, you can be linked up with the series of activities in your organization, to monitor and be in the light of the activities around. Gone are the days that, staff register, withdrawal slip, monitoring are done by individuals, e.t.c. But now, without the approval or the authentication of your biometrics, you may not be able to have an access into organization, without cards, both credit

and debit cards, you might not be able withdraw or credit an account in place other than the banking hall. Also, with the aid of camera being connected with the monitors and other tools, you can easily see various staff members at their work points, visitors coming in and out, and monitor many other things. Though we still experience the incident of fraud and other various activities in the organization and around, but there is no doubt that these have gotten extremely dwindled in their occurrences. However, security and control cannot be evaluated without evaluating the importance and contribution of the technology and innovation to be part of their agents for sustenance.

CHAPTER NINE

TIPS ON THE MEASURES THAT ENCOURAGES SECURITY AND CONTROL

This segment is to briefly expatiate and elucidate on the circumstances that improve on the security and control of an organization. To clearly state that, having a tight and well-structured security and control are visible and attainable when some certain things are fully considered. Some of the views that can be looked into are thus stated;

1. Understanding of Ourselves: This is the act of understanding the organization and more so, the workers within it. When there is an understanding to the level at which activities and the coexistence in

any organization should be, there will be drastic reduction in the insecurity and lack of control. There must be communication, most especially with the staff in term of their welfare and resolving their grievances and payment of their benefits when due, so also, the staff should know the best channel to make the management to realize their desire and expectation without being violent.

2. Understanding of the Environment: This means that people should know what they are working for or the mission of the organization and what they stand to gain thereof. When people realize what the mission of the organization looks like, they tend to give the very best to achieve at all cost, most especially, when they

know that they stand to gains at the long run and can depend on the decision of the organization as regards their promises and position to give immediately what they stand to gain. This sometimes affects the reasoning of the worker on the issues that emanate security and control at free will.

3. Consideration of people's Interest: Instead of the chief concern of the organization at all times to be exploitation and coming forth with the harsh policies, there must be consideration of the worker's interest. This is quite necessary to make a normal atmosphere in an organization. Just as illustrated beforehand, while the organization is looking out for how to meet up with her

target, the workers that are the tools for achieving the aim and ambition should not be left out not to be taken care.

4.   Respect of Law and Order: Laws and order are not what any human should tamper with unnecessarily. Any policy of an organization that has to do with certain issue or the other must not be toyed with. There must be strict action backing up policies and regulations without minding who and who are violators, and any clause that does not apply to A must not be applied to B. This makes the security and control aspect of an organization to be at the very apex of standards, and as soon as any one violates the standard or prevailing law, he is made to visit the consequences. This means

that, law enforcing is relevant in attaining the height of good security and control.

5. Free Haring and Unbiased Judgment: Whenever anyone is caught up of any indecency or an act violating the standard of an organization, or in any other criminal or fraudulent act, he must be made to appear before a panel for a fair hearing. Sometimes, the hidden aspect of the fraud and crime are more substantial than what we can measure base on what we can see or notice. There must be an avenue to allow the suspect or the fraud star to explain some certain issues which are not revealed at the point he was caught. This can however extend the scope of security and control in the organization of discourse and in the other

organization both now and the in the nearest future.

6.   Living in Unity and as one: Average human being spends their lives and time with their colleagues more than their family. In a situation of this nature, it is then advisable for such individuals to have a cordial relationship which should go beyond ordinary the working environment. When the unity and relationship in the midst of the staff are encouraged and made, it makes some secret to be known ordinarily before they are turned to an issue. Also, when they are turned to issue, they become a simple issue to find a solution to. This is as a result of the cordiality and relationship that would have made the staff to know

more of themselves in term of knowing the family members, houses or residential places, phone members and other related particulars of each other. This tends to reduce the lope hole in security and control of an organization and allows everyone to be in the position of attaining a secured environment.

7. There must not be sentiment on religion: An organization is just like a school that all forms of religion are entertained and made to work hand in hand to resolve at redeeming a purpose as proposed by the organization. It is not advisable for religion to stand as a sentiment to the working environment or to the decision of the organization. The philosophy of the organization is quite

different from that of the religion, so, the philosophy should be made more approved in the context of the conduct of her workers. This however brings about a united workers striking for a common purpose which also have an impact in how to attain the gazette of the organization, and the aspect of security and control that exist at the same time.

8. Good leadership (management): A good leadership knows of his followership and can easily relate with each of them on the same basis to come forth with his conclusive information to attain a specific project. A good leadership is quite essential to have a good measure of security and control in an organization. Without having a quality leader that is

willing to be part of his team and to be involved in the activities surrounding his mission and commitment, there might be difficulties in having a standard security and control.

9.   Good Followership (staff): it will not be too prudent to think all over on the leadership without understanding the need for a good followership. The leader can only know little of the needs and the desire of the followers. Also, when the followers form a unit or are cooperative in their decision, it might be too difficult for the leader to know the atrocity or hazard in plan. It is quite very not often for the entire followers to turn away from the authority, but when the few in control of some sensitive aspects are working

together to perpetrate their intention, it might be difficult to get to know of it. A good follower however is quite very relevant while looking into the issue of security and control in any organization in the world.

10. Issues are to be discussed and resolved amicably: Any related issues in line with the organization are to be well managed, to be discussed when due and there must be a general standard which must be applied to every single staff either now or in its future occurrences. When the issues are handled based on personal relationship or being delayed, it will surely have a significant negation on the solidity of the security and control.

11. Obedience to the Authority: Who is the authority? These are the governing body or the set of individuals or groups that makes provision for the policies and rules and regulation of an organization. The standing position is the conclusion of the authority in relations to the forwardness and growth of the organization, and this must however be well managed and appropriately discharged towards its purpose. The authority should not bend for anyone, inclusive of the set of the individual that had made it. Everyone must be responsible and bend to the authority till it is amended. This approach has a greater value on security and control.

12. Freedom of Expression must be welcome: virtually all the points are interwoven; this point is however analyzing the act of entertaining the minds and views of the employees. Though, the setting of an institution or organization should be based on forceful application of her intervention in the sense that, the workers are not permitted to change the provisions and policies, but to be compelled to move in accordance with the policies. This should however not prevent the organization to abstain from the free hearing of the worker's plight and views cum suggestion ones in a blue moon. When minds are expressed, if at all there is nothing the management has to do to the expression, it affords the employees more of the sense of belongingness and to be part of the

organization, this tend to reduce their feeling on the aspect of thinking as if they are not too relevant or otherwise to be engaged in the unnecessary acts that can be injurious and devastating to the upgrade and development of such an organization.

13.   Continuous Upgrade and Development: When people are exposed to a continuous upgrade and development, they tend to see better of their significance and values. The more you upgrade or develop yourself, the more expensive you are, and sincerely, at the point at which a man recognizes his worth at full, there are certain things he will never want to be associated with. However, on the course of security and

control, continuous upgrade and development are quite pivot to have a tangible and substantial report and result.

14. Orientation and Training: When the member staff of an organization are made to be orientated and go through training that can make them to be in the light of what they stand to gain in the nearest future as a result of doing a certain thing or the other, they are all in connection to the upliftment of such organization, the workers are more tuned and inclined with the prospect of working to get more involved in giving the best to achieve at all cost in line with what they have been exposed to, and the impression given, automatically cater ports them to their destination. This however makes the

polluted view of the employees to be transformed and neutralized, to be stream lined to the genuine pivot importance of their mission, and to be in the full understanding of what they have to gain on the management objective.

15. There must be good policy: A good policy does not only affect the life of the organization, but it also gives improvement to the welfare of the workers. It is very essential for an organization to have a good policy that can stand in defense of her workers on the future benefit and provisions for better days. A good policy will without no doubt be a need for a good security and control in an organization. When policy is softened and friendly in nature to move

the internal, mental and physical worth and value of men to give the best to have the greatest result, these affect their lives positively and has a huge effect on the life of the organization in term of security and control.

16.   Race, tribe, status, sex, language etc must not be a barrier: In an organization with a standard yard stick to operate, and an organization that is looking out for how the best can be attained, to have a coordination and control through the intimacy that should exist and the code of rules and regulation in existence must never create a barrier in term of race, tribe, status, sex, language and so forth. An organization that is willing to soar to the realm of no limitation must be above

the undue barriers of the enlisted characteristics. What this implies is that, race, language, status, sex, e t c. of a man must not make him to be treated in a manner other than how every other workers are treated. Irrespective of the nature of the man or woman in quote, he or she must have the full privilege and right of order as any other employee in an organization in question. When there is cordiality and absence of sentiment and differentiation, things tend to work in synergy and as planned to meet up with the stated ambition and this as well affect the organization in term of her control and security.

17.   People must be cultured with the mind of service: I explained orientation

and continuous learning in the topic before now. The type of program and view I was trying to analyze is not only what was covered therein. Apart from the ideology of making the employees to know the importance of the job or the essence of being employed and relating on the benefits they have to gain as a result of their contribution, it is very imperative also to make them to be cultured of the mind of service. Service is defined as an act of going miles to deliver ordinary in an extra ordinary manner to attain the business development plan and the objectives in relation to the organization. It is a way at which an encounter of an employee during the course of rendition of his function affects the genuine feeling of the customers to have the feeling of coming again for such services. Therefore, when the employees possess the kind of the nature of mind while discharging their responsibility, the tendency of having a wrong impression and fallen a victim of insecurity or laxity in control will definitely be minimal.

18.   Company's transparency and analysis: There is very crucial need for a company in her dealing to be very transparent and analytical while entering or having a contract or dealing with her member staffs and her customers. When the position of the organization is well understood and appropriately interpreted by the employee, most of them will not work or act in a wrong manner, since they know that the agreement in which they operate should not be violated. An

organization must not be greedy or too keen about herself all alone without minding the set of individuals that makes it possible for her existence and productivity and at the same time, the kings, who are the customers.

19. There must be supervision: Supervision is an act of looking after and checking various activities that are happening, before happening, while happening or after they have taken place. When there is supervision, there will not be only enlargement in the productivity, but people will also be cautious of what they do not to be made as scape goat. Also, the unnecessary transactions that are illicit in nature are exposed before they are taken place, while they are

taking place or immediately they are undertaken. Supervision plays a major role in having a substantial control and security in the organization and it must be handled carefully in a specified periodic time.

20. Good remuneration and incentive: Since the means of livelihood of all workers and employee most at times lie on what their remuneration and incentives are, mostly when they can not save or invest for the onward multiplication of such finance/fund in the organization they work or in any other organization that needs financial loan or capital to move to the next level or to make provision for a parallel part time business that can run along with what

they do in the organization at which they work, then, there is need to organize a good package that can take care of their wants and desires. A good remuneration and incentives will encourage the employees to work relentlessly and not only that, but to understand the weight and worth of what they receive not to violate the rules and regulation in connection with the organization, mostly, when they are well paid. When they can jump over the stage of starvation and lack which often triggers human subconscious to the fraudulent act or the inability to withstand temptation, falling victim of circumstance of fraud will be quite slim. However, security and control is directly connected to how good people are recompensed and paid after the discharge of their responsibility.

21. Quest for Control and Security Alertness: Just like the information given beforehand, that is, orientation and continuous learning, there must be an avenue at which people are made to know what are the things that buttresses to the control and security that we are taking about, there must be lectures on the type of the gaps in the security and control of the other organizations, there must be suggestion to the remedy and solutions, there must be alertness in the mind of the employees of the need to be cautions at all times, the penalty and the disciplinary actions must be made known, so also the other things in connections with security and control that are expected by the organization must be

strictly analyzed. It has been studied; most people forget warning so soon immediately they are pleased with their need. The point remains that, when people are reminded, they tend to guide themselves and rejuvenate their zeal to be more careful and cautious on their dealings, most especially in the issues in relation with the standard of their organization. Having the quest for the control and security alertness can however bring the gap in line with the security and control to the barest minimum level.

22. There must be till or impress account: The money for the operational purpose in the organization must not be taken from the major account of the

organization. The idea of till and impress account is to minimize the exposure of the company's cash at hand position to those who are not the approved authority and signatory to the account, or who are not in custody of it. It is to make sure that, it is not always one should go into the strong room or into the bank account for smaller or little financial requirement. The idea is to extract a certain amount of money out of the company's account, keep it in a safe with the cashier who is responsible for the disbursement and the details of collected cash to balance the account up daily before he orders for another. The lower the amount of money at hand turns to be the lower in the risk that the organization is prone to. Managing a till or impress account can however stand as an avenue to control the security and to have a control measure in an organization.

23. Cash must not be exposed to both customers and employee: it is a very bad conduct to expose the available cash in till or in the custody of any of the staff member in charge of it to the sight of the other member of the staffs, the employees or the customers who are not directly connected or authorized. There is need to have a secret on the amount or the value of money in the organization for security reason. The exposure of the people to the physical cash often leads their minds towards different intentions, most especially when they are not yet naturally matured or mentally grown. Hence, there must be regulation on the

exposure of the company's cash in till or fund at each a point in time for security and control purposes.

24. Documents and Instrument or cash related instrument must be well kept: Just like the physical cash, there are some information that can strictly reveal the position and the status of the organization at a point in time. There are a lot of things that are cash equivalent or representation which can easily be converted to cash. All these documents and instruments are meant to be well kept under lock so as to prevent the employees that are not authorized or approved, and the customers to have access to them. This often serves as a means of having a vital secret of the

organization in term of the numbers of the signatories, who and who should sign, amount of the confirmation, the processing standard and many more of the information pertaining to the organization standard. Having this in good position makes the documents and instruments to be well managed to attain the security and control at its peak.

25. Installation of Cameras and Other Monitoring gadget: in this present stage and age at which atrocity and menace of distraction and insecurity emerge, installation of camera and other monitoring gadgets are quite very essential and necessary to be in place to check on the activities around, and to monitor the affairs of the organization

without moving from a point to another. Technology has made this to be very convenient through the use of cameras that transmit to the system or desk top or hanged for the monitoring purpose. Mostly, the cameras are cleaner compare with what a mere sight can see when they are authentic. Installation of these gadget at the strategic places and around the corner of the organization curbs the series of misconduct and wrong acts which are directly associated with the insecurity and lack of control in an organization.

26. There must be restriction and out of bound at sensitive places: There must be some special areas and places which ordinary person should be restricted, guided and refrain to have access to in an

organization. When there is no restriction, there is a porous security for free entry and exit of the customers and staff which therefore leads to the highest state of insecurity. There must be a specific access information and codes for the few approved and authorized individuals that should have the permission to the entry and exit of such a sensitive places. In each time of entrance, a register must be signed by anyone that moves in, who must reveal the time and the purpose of such an action. When there is regulation of this kind, this in return leads to a tightened security and control in its own magnitude in the organization.

27.   Huge amount should not be kept over might and there must be limit to the

available physical cash: I am only trying to check on the value of money that should be left over in the safe keep over the night in the organization and the limit which must attract the attention of the cash officer to either move the excess cash to the financial institution or call on the bank for evacuation. Though, with the use of cashless operation or policy, it is expected of the organization not to transact with physical cash anymore, but due to the level of literacy in the society, many still find it conductive to transact with physical cash. It is however of need to have a specific amount of money that should be kept in the organization at a point in time. This means that as soon as the limit is crossed over, there must be movement to the bank, so also, there must be a limit that should be kept overnight in the organization, but which can be contradicted when the situation arise. This must lead to the approval by the authority in charge with a genuinely excuse established and proven. This may contributes to the decrease in the level of the insecurity and upright control in an organization.

28. Full armed men for security: In a situation at which there is cash transaction in large order. There is need for such an organization to have in its premises the presence of the security men that are well armed to secure such an organization. This might not really stand as a total prevention and guide against insecurity, but this will surely have its quota to reduce the level of insecurity

intimidation. It is never all the armed robber or evil perpetrator that have all what it takes to possess sophisticated weapons, the presence of the armed security men will however scare them away. An instance of this nature can be mentioned to be part of what gives strength and part of elements that induces a good security and control in the organization.

29. Security door and mental detecting tools are mandatory: Though, we have recorded several situations at which the mental doors were not well set and as a result of this, weapons were permitted into the operations hall and offices. Sincerely, if we have a competent hand that knows how to regulate the door, and

a good hand that understands the operation of the mental detecting tools properly, this can lead to the absolute reduction in the risk at which the organization is being confronted. Security trapdoors and mental detecting tools are to screen individual or customers not to have anything metallic in their possession while moving into the transition offices. This act can however impede the entrances of things like gun, cutlasses, machetes etc. which can be used by the notorious men to intimidate at the point of carrying out their devious act.

30. Use of hot line: most of the organizations handle the issue of hot line carelessly. Candid speaking, this had assisted thousands of many organization

in term of calling on a distress help to the issue of both internal and external aggression and hazards. Use of hot lines should be inculcated into the life of the organization such that, the entire workers and employees understand the need of it and not only that, but to have the directories of various quarters such as control unit, security units, not within the organization, police station, fire station, hospitals etc. Having a link with these set of the offices can be of a greater help at the point at which the unforeseen issues emanates. This has however added up to the control and security in its real value and context in an organization.

31. Use of exit: Having a space for the use of organization without having an exit

in it can be very dangerous. For a reasonable place to be used for an organization or transaction purpose, there is need to have nothing less than 2 doors, which must be the main entrance and exit. Though, it is always good to have more than one exit, but with the use of land and properties in the African countries in line with their stinginess and not conforming to the scales and yard stick of the properties, an exit can be welcomed. The exit can be used for different purposes, and it must be identified and known only by the employees. If possible the exit should be opened or managed by someone who must be fully ready and at alert to open it when there is cause for doing so. The exit must be channel to another place other than where the entrance is located for the escape purpose. When Provision is made for an exit, this also reduced the risk of the organization at the time of fire outbreak, robbery, etc.

32. Understanding of signage, beckoning and special languages: This can be said to be an avenue to communicate by the specific individuals, most especially the members of the staff in a way that every other person other than staff member can not decode. As stated, it can be in signage, beckoning and in special languages to pass across information. This can be an instance of covering confidential issues and at the same time, making alertness or creating awareness when certain activities are to be undertaken without making the external

people to be in the light of it. This allows the employees to conversate easily of the confidential issues without minding the presence of the crowd or customers.

It also stands as a means of giving directory and order to the subordinate either to act on a specific transaction or not without the knowledge of the person involved. There are thousands of things that can be coded and made into simple language, sign and beckons that can not be understood by any external individuals outside the circle. This also forms the act of improving on the standard of the control and security of the organization when such a special traits are in existence.

33. Signature verification: This is one of those things that most of the organizations take for granted most at times. Sincerely, many organizations have liquidated as a result of their nonchalant attitude on the issue of signature verification. It is extremely needed to verify who a staff of an organization is having any relationship with in term of his specimen of signature, most especially, when such a transaction has to do with collection of commodity, cash or any other valuable things. Each man is mandated with a particular way of identifying himself through his signature, and this must be obtained at the very beginning of any transaction or issue to be negotiated. This signature however stands as identification for the client at any point of his contact with the

organization in question. Mind you, it is very possible we have two identical twins, but their signatures must not be similar to identify them. Being careful at the point of signature verification however increases the control and the security in the organization since there may never be two signatures having the same features even when they look closely alike.

34. Proper identification is required: As soon as a client keeps on coming frequently, he is identified and his document as regards his passport and other needed requirements will definitely be in the archive of the organization, which means, it might not be too needful to be afraid of the personality one is dealing with. But in relation with the

work-in customers, there is need to have all identification required taken, to have a full detail and clue on who the organization is relating with at the course of her business transactions most especially it has to do with a sensitive transaction. Transaction must be made to the level of completion, that is, to be able to trace it back to the person in connection with it. Take for instance; "A" was sent to collect money on behalf of his boss, and "B" was there present at the point of giving the instruction to "A". Both "A" and "B" work with the client, and they both have identification card recognizing them as a staff. The client, who is their boss had already given an authority that someone will come from his company, but "B" being mischievous got to the organization to collect the commodities or cash before "A" and took it away. If proper identification has not been made, it will be extremely difficult to identify who was responsible. A proper identification traces back the transaction to the person that had related on the transaction, though a gap had been created, there will definitely be an avenue to have a remedy to the trace of the issue when an appropriate identification is in place. Hence, proper identification is required for security and control of any establishment or organization.

35. All transactions must be adequately documented: Most a times, people operate with verbal authority and requirements. Transactions should be well documented irrespective of what

kind they are. This gives transaction a trace in the processing journal of the organization. There must be ticket, receipts, books, entries and other things which must be in place to have a good documentation of the activities in the organization. Also, the documentation of all the requirements of the transaction from the client is extremely compulsory too when it has to do with the nature of the business that are mandated by the provisions or regulations. When transactions are documented, they give the right of order to the tracing of such transaction without the presence or consideration of any limitation. Without documentation of transaction, there will always be an issue on the physical cash, stocks and the properties of the organization. Therefore, all transactions must be well documented at the point of being undertaking to have a standard control and security.

36. Use of mercury light and fake notes detector: In a situation whereby cashing transaction is high or the major concern, there is need to have mercury lights and the false notes detector in place, to check the originality and the authenticity of the cash and cash representatives. Often, fake notes and instrument look so real and might be difficult to be detected by mere sight or someone that does not acquit with them. Use of mercury light and fake notes detector however makes it very easy for the processor to know that such instrument is not real. Organizations have experienced a lot of retrogression,

regression and wastages as a result of their inadequacy to have gadgets or tools to be used by their cashiers available, to guide against unnecessary loss of cash due to fake notes and instruments. There is need to make provisions for the avenue of detecting the fake presentation of all sorts of cash and cash related instruments or payment other than looking for the remedy after damage is done. Prevention is always better than cure. Mercury light and fake notes detectors are very relevant in a situation at which most of the transactions are made in cash of all sorts. i.e. NGN, USD, GBP, EURO etc. This however has its significant value and worth on the security and control in the context of the organization in question.

37   Checking of staff extravagancy attitude: Once in a while, it is always of need to check into the life of the workers, but this must not be done in an unprofessional and offensive way. Staff should be well monitored when they are growing extravagantly or spending wastefully. Most at times, the money people have not worked for are wasted extravagantly because of the pain they failed to go through before having it. It is however very imperative to take into consideration the spending habit of the staff stylishly, in a manner that will not impair their legitimate right or human right or constitute violation to worker's right of working with such an organization in which they have found themselves. This also leads to a control and security of an organizations and it might be one of

the most difficult experimentation to do not to truncate the right of the workers.

38. Pay attention to know your customer (KYC) and know your staff (KYS): This is very relevant to ascertain a good standard of security and control. Knowing the customer and staff are very necessary to have a good operation that is more than a mere operation, but which extends to knowing better of the life of both the customers and staff, that is, KYC and KYS. This is the way by which both customers and staff are known beyond the transactional office capacity. This is an attempt to know more about the customer and staff which often leads to knowing the relative of the customers and staffs. This makes it very easy to get in

touch with the relatives and next of kin of both the staff and customer when the need be, and at the same time, it creates an avenue to trace them back to their immediate environment or people and their places of living. This entails the management to pay a visit to the addresses specified by the staff or the customer and to make sure that the people living around the environment know that they are part of the environment. A good KYC and KYS can give the organization a good report of the customers and staff when it is perfectly undertaken. Hence, this is a means of having a good control and security in the organization where KYS and KYC are paramount.

39.   Prevention of loose information by the staff on the sensitive matters: Staff of the company or an organization must be trained to the level of knowing what it entails to have confidentiality in place. It is not all what they need to do as a body in an organization or the secret of the company or the useful information that must be discussed in the presence of any how individuals or the set of individuals not enclosed within the circle of association. There must be some issues that must be kept secret and confidential in term of its exposure to the public or the unapproved individuals.

Such issues ranges from the financial position, financial transaction, business development plans of the company, source of income and revenue, the tricks in use for productivity, customers information, etc. All these are meant to be well kept away from the unauthorized individuals that can make use of the information to work against the future benefit and the wellbeing of the organization. When information are well managed, the control and security become tightened up and strong.

40. Security and control must be conceived possible and tactics and approaches must be in place to attain it. There is nothing in life without no remedy to their prevailing and unforeseen problems. When a solution is not yet found for an issue, it looks as if there is none for it. Without having a mindset that the security and control are possible, one

might not be able to form the tactics and approaches that can make difference. One thing is to conceive it, and another thing is to know that it is very possible to do it. When an organization can see it plainly at the point of having it accomplished, then the required tactics and approaches can be made to overcome the insecurity and lack of control. In order way round, while preparing for the measures of the security and control, there must be preparedness to have it. It must not be something of mouth or something that can not be made hypothetical or practicable, but something that an organization can see happening and achievable to be accomplished. This however then leads to an instance of the expectation of security and control in any organization of discourse.

41. The control and security agents must be learned: when a control officer or security is not learned, he finds it extreme difficult to manage information and to draw up a chart that can lead to the excavation and detecting of the wrong acts. Security and control is a thing of the mental efficacy and reasoning ability. A control and security personnel must be at alert, and must be able to manage the activities that precedes an event to know the gap created, how it emanates and to find a lasting solution to its occurrence in the nearest future. Security and control has to do with the intelligent quotient of a man in the sense that, it is something that must be demonstrate in nature by the

application of both informal acquired knowledge and experience. Without the security and control being able carry out what they are meant to do, there might not be relevance of it. It is important to know that, when the security and control of the organization is porous, such an organization run towards her down fall and liquidation. Therefore, it is very crucial for the officers in charge to be well learned of what it takes to have security and control, and must be able to apply it on the purpose at which it was made. When the security and control system is above the loop-hole of the insecurity; the insecurity finds no place to hide. This automatically ushers the organization to the height or standard nature of operating at a realm above the insecurity and lose control.

42. Equality before law: Just same way the word equality sounded, everyone in connection with an organization must be treated equally. This means that at the point of violation, the punishment that is set must be parallel, which means, if anyone falls victim of inconsistency, his position must be disregarded for the punitive act. When the policies are rigid and inflexible on the matters in relation with the security and control, people tend to buckle up their belt and conduct not to go in contrary. By so doing, the control and security are made up and more empowered in the organization structure.

43. The security agent must be screened and of a good personality report and repute: Without having a clean hand, it might be difficult to be strict or act in accordance with the standard and policy that are guiding the issues of security and control in an environment. A security that was captured selling the property of the organization by the staff member might not be able to act accordingly when an issue of violation of law or regulation arises, most especially by the set of individuals that had caught him red handedly in the time past stealing or violating the code of conduct of such an organization.

Security and control officers are meant to be disciplined and straight forward minded individuals to be able to discharge their duty accordingly as stated by the policy of the organization. A good personality and reputation of the agents of the security and control are however very crucial and of great worth at the expense of having a good control and tight security in the organization.

44. Relevant information from the misconduct should serve as weapon: What this means is that, there must be a panel looking into any issue in relation to misconduct or wrong doing in line with security and control. Most of the organizations sack their staff immediately they get to know that they are connected with a mischievous act or being engaged with any financial misappropriation or embezzlement. This should not be the

first thing immediately any havoc is noticed of any staff, but to order for his arrest or impede him of his movement by the security agents. Through this means, we have seen a lot of the criminals confessing and returning the organization money as soon as they are caught as a result of their timidity and were sacked as soon as the money is retrieved. The whole essence of all effort to have the stolen properties, fund or asset should be more paramount compares with the intention of extermination or sacking the offender. What I am saying here is that, a panel must be in place for all form of misconduct to trace the impact, location and other individuals, e t c. in relation to any defiant or inappropriateness of conduct to be able to retrieve part of the stolen properties or fund if not all, before the due punitive act is given. This intimidation however makes more of the relevant information to the unforeseen events and upgrade in the existing policies. When someone who had made a way or penetrate through the security and control is made not to reveal his tactics and systematic approach of having it done, such a gap in the system might not be sealed off. It is very crucial for the relevant information from the notorious composed individual to be extracted before giving the due punishment. This avenue gives a better strength to the security and control not in the organization but in the organization of the world at large.

45. Smartness and swiftness: Apart from being learned, of good intelligent quotient and being able to reason, there is need to be smart and swift to be able to curb the insecurity and laxity in control. Smartness and swiftness are essential to making the act of security and control working. Steps must be taken at the right time to challenge the issue of disorderliness or misconducts. When sluggishness is formed to be part of the security and controls, there will always be a huge devastation and destruction before being noticed and regulated. To have a good security and control, it is however very necessary to understand what smartness and swiftness have to contribute to the issues revolving around the insecurity of an organization. Smartness and swiftness are pivot in making a solution or having

an end to the insecurity state and the lapses that constitutes degeneration and regression in the organizations of the world.

CHAPTER TEN

CONCLUSION

Conclusively, the book has been trying to look at the various demands that leads to porous finance, asset, and stock, and the gaps that tends to eliminate the organization and exterminates the good foresight and the intention of most of the organization in the West African and in the world at Large in which Nigeria is not excepted.

So far on the journey, we have been able to cross examine the term security and control by giving diversified introduction and definition to them. I tried to make it understood that, the term security is not only relevant to the cash and finance but to the situation and the activities in the world at large. This was said to be an act of guiding and keeping away from the devastation of the unforeseen event and circumstances.

I was able to talk briefly on what stability means in the context of the life and existence of an organization. The need to experience a stable environment in an organization before the paste for advancement can be at gain and attained, and the necessary things that brings about stability.

Also, I tried to check what brought about competition? Why the need to compete? What makes an organization to be competitive? And many more thought in relative to what the meaning of the team connotes. Any organization that fails to be competent enough to withstand others or swerves in the distorting and instable economy to have the necessary adjustment ends up suddenly with her vision and desire. Competition can simply be viewed in the aspect of the increase in productivity, meeting with the demand and the desire of the customers and increase in the innovation and technological aspects of her scope. Without these stated attributes, it might be very cumbersome if attainable to have a competition with the other industries or organization when the issue of security and control is in absinthial.

Furthermore, we looked into the gaps that are created by the lose security and control in total diasporas and the areas that needs an attention of security and control in an establishment. I was trying to say that, it might be totally difficult to nullify insecurity and to have total control in an organization. We record issue of frauds and other devastating issues in various organizations from time to time, and yet, with the fact that there is improvement in each day on security and control portfolio and findings, it has not totally eradicated the issue of insecurity and lapses in control, but a proper standard that should make an organization not to be a bad exemplary should be managed.

I tried to also look into the consequence and outcome of the insecurity and laxity in control, looking at the different and regression it contributes to the growth and development of an organization. These outcomes and consequences however are the major causes of the predicaments most of the organization experiment in term of their growth and development, productivity, increase and expansion, and having an accurate brain storming that brings about a radical change and transformation etc.

The book also tried to review the agent of security and control in an organization. This simply implies that, security and control might not be able to stand or be experimented without certain crucial and important agents that must be considered prior to the issue of security and control. There must be a certain place or captioned segment that must be defined, and a standard must be in place to measure the security and control in a certain condition or the other to evaluate the application or the end result of its effects. When a particular place is defined, then, the components that are synonymous to the environment and the condition within the specific captioned portion can however be evaluated. In nut shell, security and control might not be visible without the agents that are involved in it. The last overview in the book was what brings about security and control. Here, I was looking at what are the factors to be considered to have a minimal insecurity and weakened control in an organization. Some of the necessary and crucial things that ranges from several thought are however enlisted and briefly expatiated to the readers.

This topic or issue is however very vast and wide in the sense that, having a long note or a book bigger than this might not be able to make the important of the solution well analyzed and experimented. This is supposed to be more hypothetical than theoretical. The essence of this topic is to outline and figure out the various barriers in relation to security and control in an organization and to quench the level of decadence and destruction that is over throwing the standards in practices. It is very pivot to have a better clue and understanding of what is takes to have a good security and control in an organization, but, it is much more expedient to have the trait and configuration of the security and control in practice to save the storm and uproar that often constitute instability or rather capsizes most of the organizations in the world.

Since I understood that, reading alone might not be sufficient, I have tried to inculcate the idea of organizing seminars, training, consultation, and interactive sessions and to be involved in business resources strategies and control as my service. I am of the optimistic mind that this advance attempt to go further to establish a factual standard and position to strangle the insecurity and the gaps in the control and security will definitely go a long way in the cause of total eradication of the financial misappropriation, embezzlement, fraud, robbery attacks, wastages, illicit property acquisition and conversion of organization property, and other attacks on the organizations to be stabilized and competitive in their regular daily dealings and undertakings in all region and places where businesses are enveloped in the world at large.

CONTACTS

TOPE ADENIJI

+234-803-718-4404 OR +234-808-093-5806

tophyeva@yahoo.com   NIGERIA, WEST-AFRICA.

REQUEST AND SOLICITATION

The development of the world at large begins in the respective economic function and the input of the organizations and individuals, therefore, there should be measures that can provide adequate security and control to create enabling environment at which the economic function can be effective.

We solicit that some of these books should be downloaded on individual basis or order for the bulk purchase of the printed copies.

So also, you can be of support with your suggestion, constructive criticism and financially.

Thank you immensely.

www.ingramcontent.com/pod-product-compliance
Lightning Source LLC
Chambersburg PA
CBHW020632220526

45464CB00001B/118